the
property
pension
plan

Financial Freedom Through
Buy To Let Investment

Paul Mahoney

RETHINK PRESS

First published in Great Britain in 2019 by Rethink Press (www.rethinkpress.com)

© Copyright Paul Mahoney

Cover image © Shutterstock | antkevyv

Praise

'This book explains in great detail a tried and proven approach to wealth creation that is under-utilised: property! Anyone interested in making and/or storing wealth, whether it be in property or otherwise, should read it. 5 Stars!'
> — John Howard, landlord, property developer and author with 40 years' experience

'As we're accustomed to on Property TV shows that Paul hosts and features in, in this book he explains wealth creation and property investment in easy-to-understand terms and makes it accessible to everyone. I highly recommend this book!'
> — Michael Hammond, CEO of Property TV and Entrepreneur of the Year 2018

'We have worked with Paul over numerous years and he always delivers great seminars at our National Landlord Investment Shows. Paul's experience has helped so many, from new investors to seasoned landlords, grow and retain their portfolios. I am sure that this book will help educate you on your property journey.'
> — Tracey Hanbury, Director at The National Landlord Investment Show

'Clear, concise and insightful, Paul's passion for helping others achieve financial freedom through property investment shines through in this easy to read, step-by-step guide. I only wish this book was around when I started out!'
— Joe Billingham, founder and CEO of Prosperity Wealth

'Fantastic content covering all major buy to let investment principles. Great for investors of all levels wishing to further their knowledge and take their investments to the next level. Paul's depth and breadth of knowledge is superb and his book is a must read!'
— Nicholas Wallwork, CEO of PropertyForum. com; investor, developer and author of *Investing in International Real Estate For Dummies*

'This book is the new "go to" reference for property investment for the future. We, at LH1 London, act as sales and marketing partners for developers, as well as property investors ourselves. We believe "property is our pension" and with our grandchildren's future to consider, we totally endorse Paul Mahoney of Nova Financial's philosophy and forward-thinking knowledge of the property investment market.'
— Rayna Hunter, Director of LH1 London Ltd

'A *must* read for anyone looking to build true wealth from property investment. A straight forward and proven formula from one of the industry's most respected experts, Paul Mahoney. As global sales and marketing consultants on some of the UK's most prolific residential developments, LH1 London only work with trusted partners; Paul and Nova Financial are certainly one of our most valued. Paul has worked tirelessly to open the door of strategic property investment to the masses and this book is certainly testament to all his efforts and hard work.'

— Benjamin Hunter, CEO of LH1 London Ltd

'Given my experience across regulated financial services and property in the UK and abroad for over 20 years, investing into income producing assets wins hands down, which Paul and Nova's wealth creation model clearly demonstrates in this compelling read. Like all things Nova do, this book is excellent!'

— Gary Powell, Property Developer, Founder of Admired Properties

Contents

Introduction

According to *The Guardian* Newspaper in 2017, one in seven people retiring that year relied solely on a maximum potential state pension of just £151.25 per week – but 63% of people will receive less than that. In Moneywise news in January 2018, a think tank predicted that the state pension pot will run out in twenty years, and over 50% of people over the age of fifty will rely partly on it to stay afloat in retirement.

While our finances are central to our lives, many people neglect to make the best use of the money for which they work so hard. With the right tools, you have the potential to significantly improve your quality of life.

I'm Paul Mahoney, Managing Director of Nova Financial Group which provides advice on finance and property investment. I'm an experienced landlord and investor, and while I don't claim to know everything about finance, investments or property, I can help you understand the investment journey with a focus on property as an attractive asset class.

That's why I've written this book. I hope it will empower you to reach your financial goals, and show how and why property investment is the best option to help you get there. It will show you how the average 'mum and dad' investor, a person or couple living the average UK family life between the ages of thirty to fifty, can achieve success using this asset class.

The book is divided into three sections which break down the property investment journey in easy steps:

1. **Understanding You** includes understanding your current situation, setting your goals and deciding on a strategy that is suitable for you. It will also cover why most people should choose property as an investment option, what property investment is, and provide a better awareness of your financial position. Finally, you will discover the RETIRE Investment Journey, a six-step model to help you prepare for your retirement.

2. **Understanding Property** includes the Ten Fundamentals for Successful Passive Property Investment, how to finance your investments

with the right mortgage, and how to get a clearer understanding of tax structuring and rules that affect property investment and how to ensure you stick to them.

3. **Understanding Implementation** is the final section that is focused on taking action based upon what you've learned in the book and actually making positive change to your financial position. I will also cover the logistics of property investment, the importance of independent advice and how to set up a management structure to enable you to successfully manage your growing portfolio without having to get involved in the day to day detail yourself.

There are ten chapters which will lead you through the process of passive property investment. In Chapter 1 I will cover the problem with pensions and how you can use other investment options such as property investment to help you plan for your financially secure retirement. Chapter 2 discusses why property investment might be the best option for you, including what sort of returns you can get for your money. In this chapter I also cover the importance of the passive property investment model and how this differs substantially from property development. Chapter 3 is vital to your understanding of your full financial position. Here I will introduce the six steps of the RETIRE Investment Journey model which are:

- Ready to get started

- Education

- Testing the water

- Investing further

- Retirement transitioning

- Easy retirement

These steps will help you set the goals you need to build your successful property portfolio. Key to that success is research and due diligence, which I will cover in more detail in Chapter 4. Chapter 5 will give you an overview of aspects to consider when you're researching potential properties before investing. In Chapters 6 and 7 we will explore the importance of financing your investment correctly, the types of mortgages available and how to access them along with the necessary information you need regarding tax structures and accounting. Once you've begun your portfolio building, you'll want to implement the right management structure to allow you to achieve a passive investment rather than require active hands on management, and Chapter 8 will give you clear advice on how to set up the right management structure for you. Chapter 9 looks at the great opportunity that property investment provides to business owners, and finally in Chapter 10 we will discuss how you can utilise your wealth to help others who are less well-off than you both locally and globally.

Use this book as a guide to take you through the hurdles of property investment and make the journey as easy as possible. At the end of each chapter you will find questions to help you analyse and take action on the content, which is vital to beginning your property investment journey.

If you're interested in replacing your employment income with passive income generated from your investments with little effort from you – which is the holy grail of investing – then this book is for you. Did you receive any formal education on money and/ or investments in school or at home? Would you say that you're completely financially literate? Are you familiar with leveraged property investment and what it can do to help your financial situation and your ability to build financial freedom? Do you know all the things to consider and the fundamentals to apply when planning and implementing a suitable property investment strategy and selecting the right assets? If any of your answers are no or you're not sure, then this book is for you!

UNDERSTANDING YOU

Gaining a deeper understanding of you is the whole purpose of this book, and is, aside from property, one of the key outcomes I'm here to provide. The main focus of this section is on you, the reader. This section is going to help you better understand your current situation, understand the importance of goal setting and get a clear strategy for achieving those goals. Once you have that strategy, we will determine what the best investment asset class is going to be for you. You can then actually start making positive changes and work toward your goals.

Understanding You will help you set up the framework that holds the whole successful portfolio together. In the end, we don't really care about property or investments. We're not emotionally attached to the asset. Instead, we're focused on the outcomes the asset can provide, or the end goal. Everyone is different. Everyone has different current financial positions, are at different stages of life, and have different goals and different resources that enable them to achieve certain goals.

Unfortunately, some people will not achieve their goals. That's why we need to be realistic. Where many people go wrong when it comes to goal setting or investing is in seeking out get rich quick schemes and wanting more than what is actually legitimately available to them. They often take too much risk or get ripped off by unscrupulous people.

In these first three chapters we will cover all you need to know about your investment options, the issues to be aware of and help you to decide whether property is the right investment area for you.

CHAPTER ONE

The Problem

Why invest in properties? You can't rely on your pension to retire comfortably – which is why property should be considered as a vehicle for wealth and an investment tool for achieving financial goals. Pensions may be very tax effective vehicles, but the investment options in them are terrible. They are made up of large funds that generally underperform in the market, they charge big fees, and even if you put every penny you have into your pension, the returns you're going to get on that money are not going to be very good.

In this first chapter we will discuss the advantages and disadvantages of pensions, as well as the other types of investments available to you. I will answer the questions I'm asked most frequently so that you can make a more informed choice about which investments might be best for you. Let's start first by looking in greater depth at pensions.

Pensions

I am not a huge fan of pensions. Why? Well, according to a recent CNBC article: 'Here's why millennials are not investing', 80% of people work their entire lives while saving very little and they don't invest unless forced to by their employer in the form of pension contributions.[1]

Pensions are a very tax effective option for saving money for retirement and have traditionally been the go-to investment option for this reason. In the UK, you're currently able to contribute up to £50,000 per annum to your pension completely tax free, and returns generated within the pension are predominantly tax free also which, for most, is much better than having investments in your personal name and paying 20%, 40% or 45% tax on returns as part of your income (based on the current tax thresholds) and quite often capital gains tax on the sale of the investments also.

But should we all contribute as much as possible to our pension? That depends on your situation. The following are some questions to consider.

1   Weiss, J. 'Here's why millennials aren't investing'. April 2016 http://www.cnbc.com/2016/04/01/heres-why-millennials-arent-investing.html

What will your money be invested in?

Let's look at your investment options within your pension. Although options have become more flexible, pensions are still predominantly equities focused, meaning you're somewhat limited. The traditional investment options within a pension tended to be shares, bonds, and cash, mostly invested in unit trusts across diversified portfolios that depended on your risk profile and aimed to either track or outperform the market. These have historically underperformed, though there has been some progress on this which has resulted in more flexibility, such as the ability to invest in Real Estate Investment Trusts (REITS). However, these also tend to be diversified portfolios with subpar returns. There are also now options to self-manage your pension in a Self-Invested Personal Pension (SIPP) or a Small Self-Administered Scheme (SSAS), often referred to as a Director's Pension, but aside from Director's Pensions (I'll talk about these in Chapter 9) these structures are mostly still governed by platforms which restrict where the money is invested.

How and when can you take your money or draw an income?

One of the main restricting factors of a pension, especially for the more entrepreneurial investor that intends to want to retire early, is the fact that you cannot access the funds until you are at least fifty-five. Even then, you can only access 25% of your pension tax free until you are sixty years of age.[2] While all too often people are their own worst enemies when it comes to having access to large sums of money, this option is quite restrictive. If your goal is to retire earlier than fifty-five or sixty, then perhaps having the majority of your funds in a pension is not for you.

What fees do you have to pay?

Fees are important to consider. In 2016 the average pension charged fees of 1.85%. Typical fees include a yearly management fee and an exit fee. But in a study completed by the Office of Fair Trading which was referenced by Dan Hyde, Consumer Affairs Editor of *The Telegraph*, in his article called 'Pension Scandal: One in four faces rip-off fees', it was found that there were actually thirty-eight potential fees that can be charged by various pension schemes.[3] The same study found that those with smaller pension pots are charged the highest fees, which can sometimes be more than 3% per annum. This may not sound like much, but when the FTSE All Share Index is averaging circa 6%, those fees are half of your return and are often even charged if you make a loss, increasing your loss even further!

---

2   Oxlade, A. 'Cash in your pension at 55? You may have to wait till 70'. *The Telegraph*, April 2015. www.telegraph.co.uk/finance/personalfinance/special-reports/11537512/Cash-in-your-pension-at-55-You-may-have-to-wait-till-70.html
3   Hyde, D. 'Pension Scandal: One in four faces rip-off fees'. *The Telegraph*. 17 December 2014

What is the right pension for you?

There are a variety of pensions available and determining which one is right for you can be difficult. You can seek the advice of a financial advisor; however the returns are limited as your investment options are mostly conservative unit trust investments.

Assuming your pension investments do return as you expect they will, then you must consider how you access your money and what to do with it at retirement. The traditional option is to take an annuity, which is a recurring amount of income annually until your death, based on a formula that is determined by how much you invest.

For example, if you have £500,000 at retirement and take an annuity, the level of income you would receive per annum from 2018 to the year of your death would be only approximately £11,400 depending on your age, health, and a number of other risk management factors. To get to a return that gives a fairly average living cost of £40,000 per annum, you would need about £2,000,000 – which is significantly more than most people have by the age of retirement. To find out more and get a personal quote, visit the Money Advice Service at https://www.moneyadviceservice.org.uk.

This is a good arrangement for the company offering the annuity as they get access to all of your retirement funds and pay you a fixed amount each year until you die – regardless of whether they have paid you back all your money or not. The rate of return to you at the time of writing in 2018 will be less than 5% – which means if you start the annuity at sixty-five years old, then you will only get your money back if you live beyond eight-five years old, which is not a great investment. You will find further helpful information about this in 'Four solutions to the annuity problem', an article on the Unbiased website.[4]

I don't know about you, but the annuity option is not that exciting to me. Unless you have quite a lot of money at retirement, meaning you're earning a lot now and able to contribute strongly or have a big inheritance coming, it's unlikely to provide you with the income that you want and need. Added to this is the fact that the government is constantly tinkering with the pension rules, and with a general trend towards the retirement age being extended and tax concessions being made less attractive. Tying up all of your money in a pension is not a great idea, especially if you'd like to retire early.

I personally don't feel comfortable allocating the vast majority of my wealth to the whim of the government, especially with an aging population and more pressure on tax concessions for what is very loosely perceived as 'the wealthy'. Wealthy

---

4   Green, N. 'Four Solutions to the Annuity Problem'. 5 December 2018. www.unbiased.co.uk/news/financial-adviser/four-solutions-to-the-annuity-problem

is a subjective term and can therefore be used in the government's agenda to implement changes. I wouldn't define someone with sufficient funds to sustain a comfortable lifestyle without a pension as wealthy, but there are some who would. Many people would like to have a debt free home and circa £50,000 of passive income per annum. This would require an investable asset base of £1,000,000 on a 5% yield, making that person a millionaire. But should that person be punished for their hard work leading up to retirement? I think not. But I don't set government policy.

Does that mean that everyone's retirement is doomed? The naysayers would have you believe so – but there are other investment options available. I'm not saying that pensions are a bad investment and shouldn't be utilised. Absolutely not. But they also shouldn't be the only investment option as your main source of retirement funds. I recommend that everyone has a pension, if only for the tax benefits, and especially if your employer will contribute for you or add to your contributions. However, you should be aware that there are other investment options which can generate much better returns in both the asset building and retirement phases of life. Having gone more deeply into the details of pensions, we can now turn to the other investment options available to you.

Investment options

When it comes to investing, you have three broad options which are:

1. Interest bearing investments

2. Shares

3. Property

Other investments such as commodities and fine wine don't generate an income and are therefore more of a speculation with a potential for an increase in value rather than an investment. Which one is right for you? Let's look at each in turn.

1. Interest bearing options

   This type of investment includes cash in the bank, term deposits, ISAs and any other type of investment where you invest your funds and receive a fixed or variable cash flow return without the chance of the capital value of your investment increasing or decreasing (other than with inflation). You can get your initial funds back at some point in the future with interest. In general, returns tend to be approximately 2% to 4% per annum.

2. Shares

   When investing in shares you're buying a portion of ownership in a company. There are several different ways to determine which companies you should invest in, such as:

- Fundamental analysis: an attempt to measure the real value of an investment versus its current value

- Technical analysis: identifying patterns and trends in price movement and predicting what will happen next

- Trading: buying and selling stocks, ideally to make money on the difference

Or you can simply guess and hope for the best. Mostly investing in shares, this is based on an optimistic view of the prospects of that company. Often such companies will have a historical return that is made up of capital appreciation (or depreciation) and dividends, which is the yearly income provided through the share of profits. In general, historical returns tend to be approximately 6% to 8% per annum, but vary greatly across different sectors and types of companies.[5]

3. Property

This is the purchase of real estate for the purpose of letting out to tenants to generate an income, and ideally generate an increase in the capital value. The old cliché of location, location, location is very important here and often determines the demand

5   Wrigglesworth, *Buy to let comes of age.'* 2013

for a property due to employment, facilities, and amenities in an area. In the right locations, supply tends to be restricted due to land being a limited commodity and if there is a strong demand then prices tend to increase. Purchasing real estate is similar to purchasing shares in that the net return on a cash purchase tends to be 6% to 8% per annum. But the big differentiating factor with property is the ability to access finance at relatively high loan to value ratios, over the long term at low interest rates, and also that lenders have no ability to call in the loan until the end of the period. This leverages the funds invested and, assuming returns are positive, then it accelerates them.

Should you borrow to invest?

When it comes to making an investment, you must decide whether your investment will be solely a cash investment or if you plan to leverage your cash to make a larger investment. Taking on debt to invest can be higher risk, but not taking on any debt can put you at risk of not meeting your goals and under-utilising your money. Unfortunately, most people struggle to save sufficient funds over their working life for retirement, so the prudent use of investment debt is, in many cases, essential to reach their goals.

If you're investing in interest bearing investments, then in most cases borrowing doesn't make any sense.

This is because the cost of borrowing will outweigh the return and defeat the purpose.

When investing in shares, you can borrow to invest with what is called a margin loan. Margin loans work on the basis that your lending can only be a certain percentage of your portfolio value. The risk here is that if the value of your shares falls, the loan percentage increases. You can then be forced to sell at the worst time, or add more money in a falling market. Interest rates tend to be high at 6% or more at the time of writing in 2018, with the maximum loan to values (LTV) of around 60%. Borrowing to invest in shares is high risk and high cost, meaning the return you need to generate must be higher to make it worthwhile.

Property investment enables you to borrow at a low interest rate of 2% to 3% at the time of writing, for twenty years or more, with no ability for recall and at loan to value rates of 75% or greater. Low risk, low cost, and hence even an average return can actually result in a greater overall return on the cash invested, given the multiplying factors that debt provides.

For example, if you invest £25,000 in a £100,000 property, then with just a 5% increase in value, which is less than the historical average, you will get a 20% return on your £25,000 of £5,000. Assuming that your rental income is sufficient to cover and exceed your interest repayments and costs, which it usually is depending on location, then you can also add net income to your overall return.

This is the beauty of leveraged property. Fairly average returns on the overall property value can result in great returns on your cash applied. Consider the fact that you can re-mortgage properties every few years to release the equity from capital growth and invest further, as well as, pay down debt with the income, and you have a strong strategy for building an investable asset base over the long term.

The graph below shows the returns generated from key investments asset classes per annum between 1996 and 2013. Leveraged buy to let significantly outperformed all other asset classes.[6]

What have you learned?

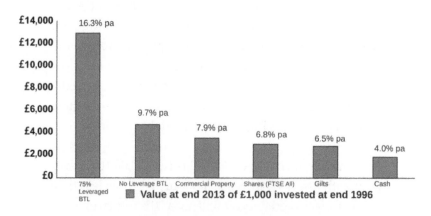

Fig. 1.1 Cumulative total returns for the main UK asset classes (1996-2013)

---

6   'Buy to let comes of age', Wrigglesworth, 2013.

Cash bearing investments provide a stable and reliable cash flow return, but they don't enable you to grow your asset base or to borrow to better utilise your money. They are mostly suitable for storing rather than creating wealth.

Shares can provide a better return than cash, but both borrowing costs and risks are high and it's difficult to justify much borrowing for most people. Shares can be suitable to storing and building wealth but without the benefits of cost effective and high loan to value leverage.

Property generally provides a similar return to shares as a cash purchase, but the borrowing enables an investor to multiply returns with a relative amount of confidence as compared with other options.

Questions for you

1. Do you currently own any of these three investment types?

2. If so, what is your allocation and is it right for you?

3. If not, which one is right for you?

4. Do you currently have borrowings?

5. If not, have you thought about this strategy and why haven't you implemented it?

6. If so, is it the right amount and type of borrowings to help you achieve your goals?

7. In the next chapter we will look at why I believe property is the best investment option for most people, and what returns you can hope to earn from your investments.

CHAPTER TWO

Why Property?

To start investing successfully in property, you need to understand the basics. Get these right and you're already on the road to success. To help you on your way, I will cover how much income you can expect to earn from your property investment, the importance of economic stability, and how it can affect your investments, as well as the principles of re-investment and liquidity.

The returns generated from leveraged buy to let property over the past twenty years have been incredible. The average return on funds invested in a buy to let with 75% leverage over twenty years to 2013 was 16.1% per annum. This greatly exceeds the returns generated by other popular investment asset classes. This is because property gives you the ability to borrow money at high loan to value rates, a low interest rate, and over long periods of time without taking too much risk and with no ability for the lender to recall the mortgage even if the value of your property falls significantly.

To borrow to invest in shares is risky, and the highest loan to value is approximately 60%, which is 40% of your own cash invested. Rates at the time of writing range upwards from 6%, and if the value of your shares fall below an accepted level then you either have to or contribute more funds. This often results in people selling at the worst possible time and losing money simply because market sentiment is low. That said, even as a cash purchase, property has outperformed the FTSE All Share Index consistently.

It's important to note that without the prudent use of investment debt, it's very difficult for the vast majority of people to achieve their lifestyle and financial goals: even if they saved most of their income, they still wouldn't have enough funds to retire and passively generate the income that they need. Make sure to assess the best use of your resources and make investments that not only fit with your risk versus reward profile, but also align with your target timeframe and current resources.

Since 1926, house prices in the UK have, on average, more than quadrupled every twenty years. Compared with the share market, the FTSE 100 is lower today than it was in 1999. You can find out more about the impact of the increase in house prices in Jefford's excellent article 'House prices soar by 47,000 per cent in the 90 years since the Queen was born'.[7]

What income can you expect?

The current average rental yield according to the Buy to Let Rental Yield Map 2018/2019 available on UK property is approximately 5%, which means that you're able to achieve approximately £1 per week per £10,000 investment.[8] For example, a £100,000 property will rent for approximately £100 a week but this differs greatly depending on location and type of property, with the range being mostly between 3% and 8%. The average growth in rental yield has been 4.2% per annum, against a historical inflation rate of 2%, which means that rents are growing at a much faster rate than people's incomes.

As opposed to many other investment types, at current interest rates of 2% to 3% it actually makes sense to borrow for income. This is due to the yield being higher than the cost of borrowing which accelerates your returns. For example, a property that is yielding 7% (2% higher than the UK average, but very achievable in the right areas) with a 75% mortgage will often provide a return on cash invested of 10% plus per annum after all

---

7   Jefford, K. 'House prices soar by 47,000 per cent in the 90 years since the Queen was born'. City A.M. 4 April 2016
8   Buy to Let Rental Yield Map 2018-2019, www.totallymoney.com/buy-to-let-yield-map

expenses have been paid and excluding any potential growth. Rents and growth are very much determined by demand, so as long as you invest in the right areas with strong reasons for people to want to live there, you can have confidence in rental demand regardless of the state of the economy as tenants still need a roof over their heads and property price growth over the mid to long term.

Comparing this to shares, the average dividend from the FTSE 100 is 4.2% and interest rates for margin loans are 6% plus. Given that the interest rate is higher than the yield, it doesn't make sense to borrow to invest in shares if your main goal is to generate income. Even if you invested in higher yielding types of shares where the yield was 6% plus, the gap would be minimal and the cash flow wouldn't be far above neutral. Average dividend growth in the FTSE 100 has been 3%, but the risk with dividends is that they can drop at the whim of management or if the company or market is not performing well. Let's look at the issue of economic stability and how it can affect your investment.

Stability

Property tends to be a more stable and reliable investment when compared to other investment options. According to Dan Stewart in his article 'House prices fall 8% in a year', during the financial crisis of 2008 UK property values fell by 8%.[9] In the same year Graham Ruddick wrote 'FTSE 100 suffers worst year ever', and states that the FTSE All Share Index fell by 31%.[10] It's important to understand how volatility and risk affect your investment.

Property is a tangible asset that, as long as it's structurally stable, cannot disappear and will therefore retain some value even in bad economic times. Even the biggest publicly listed companies can go bust and share values can go to zero in times of economic crisis. However, assuming your property is in the right location, you can have confidence that it will still rent and provide an income even in difficult times. In fact, in city centres and economic hub areas with strong employment, rents often increase in an economic downturn because there is less funding in the market for purchases and more rental pressure where jobs are focused. This is opposed to shares, where both prices and dividends tend to drop as companies cannot pay dividends if they're not making a profit.

Re-investing and liquidity

Net cash flow from property can be applied to paying down the debt, which enables the investor to reduce their loan to value ratio quicker and potentially

9 Stewart, D. 'House prices fall 8% in a year'. December 2008. www. building.co.uk
10 Ruddick, G. 'FTSE 100 suffers worst year ever'. *The Telegraph*. December 2008

re-mortgage to re-invest sooner. Property is generally a high-value asset and is often the most expensive purchase that people will ever make. This also means the application of larger sums of money to each investment, which could be perceived as a downside. A deposit in the tens of thousands needs to be saved, and there are high entry costs such as Stamp Duty and legal fees, and high exit costs like agent fees and capital gains tax. This makes property a relatively illiquid asset, which is viewed as a negative by some.

A property's illiquidity is a positive for the vast majority of people, myself included. The reason for this is that saves us from ourselves. That is, it saves us from having to watch the market to find the right time to buy and sell, and having the stomach to hold on when we can see prices fall sharply. Very few people sell their properties when they see on the news that China is having economic issues, for example. People do that with shares which results in a volatile market and often buying and selling at the wrong times. With property people tend to hold on through bad times and benefit from a recovering market.

Property – the basics

According to Richard Godwin in his article for *The Guardian* entitled 'How much do you earn? It is not something you want to talk about', the average income in the UK for a full-time employee is £28,677.[11] Based upon a 5% net yield on your investment asset base, you would need £573,540 to generate that amount in passive income. Therefore, without investing, the average employee would need to save all of their income over twenty years, or half of their income over forty years to get there, and even then the value of their money would be eroded by inflation. It stands to reason that without investing and generating positive returns it will be very difficult to achieve your retirement goals.

If you want to know how to calculate how much of an investable asset base you would need to replace your income on a 5% net yield, which is fairly achievable regardless of the state of the economy, simply divide your income by 0.05.

For example, an income of £40,000 would be:

£40,000 / 0.05 = £800,000

Therefore, the person who earns £40,000 would need an investable asset base of £800,000 on a 5% net yield to replace their income.

Passive income is income generated from investments in a way that requires little to no time from the investor. Often this style of investing is called 'arm

---

11   Godwin, R. 'How much do you earn? It's not something you want to talk about'. *The Guardian*. 2018

chair' investing, which is the opposite of being hands on and developing property or going out to fix the toilets of your properties every weekend. Investors should view property as being a box that generates money as opposed to an ongoing project.

There are two ways property can be bought:

1. Debt free property
2. Leveraged property

Debt free property is bought with cash rather than a mortgage. This is the most conservative way to buy property as there is no risk of interest rates rising, or failing to meet mortgage repayments if your property is empty.

Leveraged property is bought with a mortgage. The standard buy to let mortgage loan to value in the UK is 75%, which means that a 25% deposit is required to purchase. Leveraged property makes it possible to generate returns on a higher value asset or assets than if you were a cash buyer. Although there are risks, the access to a greater value asset or multiple assets can accelerate returns on the funds applied. Other risks include interest rates rising and meeting mortgage repayments.

Positive cash flow property is property that generates more income than all of the costs required to maintain the property, such as mortgage repayments, lettings and management, services charges and ground rent as well as maintenance. For example, a property that rents for £1,000 per month and has £700 per month of expenses is £300 per month cash flow positive. Many investors aim for cash flow positive properties even if their main focus is not cash flow, as it creates a buffer for affordability and sustainability.

Buy to let mortgages are the mortgages available for properties that are bought for the purpose of renting to a tenant. These mortgages first became available in the UK in 1996 when buy to let became very popular due to the strong returns available. Historically, interest rates for buy to let have been higher than residential mortgages, however that has changed in recent years with the increase in competition in lending, and there are now many buy to let mortgage products available at similar rates to residential mortgages.

According to the Money Facts website, 75% of buy to let mortgage rates are available at interest rates of less than 2%. Interest rates are the cost of borrowing and are referred to in percentage terms, which is the amount that you pay the lender as a proportion of the amount you have borrowed. For example, if you borrow £100,000 at an interest rate of 3%, then your yearly interest repayment is £3,000. This is if the loan repayments are on an interest only basis, whereas with principal and interest loans there is also a repayment portion over and above the interest repayments. Most buy to let mortgages are interest only, but some investors choose to take principle and interest mortgages, especially if they no longer have any personal debt (eg their home loan).

The net income of buy to let properties, which is income after expenses generated from property investment, is taxable and forms part of your yearly income for tax purposes. There are various tax strategies and ways of structuring an investment that is suitable for your situation, which is an area worth getting professional advice on if you're an active investor or planning to invest.

Expenses are tax deductible. Currently most expenses incurred in running and maintaining a property investment are tax deductible against the income generated. There are changes currently being implemented in phases called Section 24, which means that by 2020 mortgage interest will no longer be deductible, but a tax credit will be given at 20%, which is also the basic rate of tax. If you earn less than £45,000 (you're a basic rate tax payer) including property income then the changes won't affect you. If you earn more than £45,000, you own the properties in your name and you have mortgages, then property investments will be less tax efficient and you should seek advice on potential solutions. We will return to Section 24 in a later chapter, however you can find further information in the UK

Government's Policy Paper 'Restricting finance cost relief for individual landlords'.[12]

Returns from property are given in the form of income and/or capital growth. Cash flow is the rental income minus expenses, and capital growth is the increase in the property value over time. Some investors prefer one or the other depending on what they're hoping to achieve from their investment. The best choice for you depends on your stage of life and financial position and will be discussed later in the book.

Returns

In a report titled 'Buy to Let Comes Of Age' (referred to in Chapter 1),[13] it was determined that the average buy to let property that was purchased with cash generated returns of 9.7% per annum after all expenses, and the same property with a 75% buy to let mortgage generated returns of 16.3% per annum over eighteen years up to 2013. That is versus 6.8% from the FTSE all shares index and 4% from cash.

---

12 'Restricting finance cost relief for individual landlords', HMRC, updated 6 February 2017, www.gov.uk/government/publications/ restricting-finance-cost-relief-for-individual-landlords/ restricting-finance-cost-relief-for-individual-landlords
13 Wrigglesworth, *'Buy to let comes of age.'* 2013

Passive property investment, not property development

When it comes to investing in property, I really view it the same as I view any other investment option: as a means to an end, a way of better utilising your money to better contribute toward your financial freedom in the future, an early retirement, or even just a normal-age retirement but with a comfortable lifestyle.

At Nova we meet with a lot of people who want to buy and renovate, convert commercial properties to residential property, or new build property development. This is spurred on by something they've read, a TV show they have watched, or maybe a seminar they have attended. They tell us these events or shows don't help when it comes to developing property or to managing a project of such a scale.

An analogy that I often use for this is that you don't just read an article, do a course or attend a seminar and then start performing brain surgery. That's because property development is a profession not a hobby. It's something that people spend years perfecting. They learn trades and skills from other people, find out how to manage contractors to make sure they're doing the right job and deliver a profitable project. That is not something that you can learn overnight, and it shouldn't be attempted by a complete novice.

People say as there is so much money to be made in property development, why would you want to invest in property passively and achieve average returns of 5% to 10% yields and 5% to 10% growth? But those returns are on the asset value, which can result in strong total returns of 30% plus per annum on the funds applied when you are using leverage to multiply the return on deposit.

In our experience you are far better off investing passively if you don't have the expertise in property development, and I must stress that this expertise cannot be learned in a matter of days, weeks or months – but years. It's a very detailed process and I have come across far too many people who have been burnt, when taking that leap to develop property without the right experience and without the right expertise. There is just so much that can go wrong.

For example, you could go down the route of choosing a primary contractor to manage all of your subcontracts, such as an electrician, a plumber, a plasterer and all the trades that are required for a renovation or a development project. If you choose this option of having somebody else manage that for you, then that person essentially has your livelihood in their hands. You need to have absolute confidence that they're going to make the best possible choices for you to minimise cost, minimise time and deliver the most possible profit.

But how can you incentivise a contractor to do that? Firstly, you need to make sure they are trustworthy. Look at their testimonials and at what they have done in the past. But again, without any experience, are you going to do that efficiently? If you are going to manage your properties yourself, things become a lot more complex. I wouldn't recommend this.

Let's break down the items you will have to manage yourself if you go it alone. A simplified list of the tasks and skills required would be:

- Run feasibility on many site options

- Organise suitable finance if required

- Select the right site that is fit for purpose

- Manage the design process

- Be aware of planning or extra costs you might incur

- Be aware of the potential for delays and how that affects the viability of the project

- Effectively vet and select contractors and then manage them to deliver on time, at agreed cost and to spec

- Bear the risk of running into economic issues, such as a recession, halfway through your build, which might impact your funding or the stability of your contractors

- Either sell or re-mortgage once done to realise your potential profit

You can see from this list that there is much more risk involved than buying a rundown property and making loads of money. Property development is a business. It's a profession. It's very, very different to passive investing so of course you would expect to make more profit from it because you are taking so much more risk. In most renovation projects I aim to make 10–15%, and with developments up to and over 25%, however we've had clients that outperform this just by buying off plan and doing nothing. For all the success stories that you hear in this realm of property investment, there are significantly more failures, especially when you're talking about people that don't have the right experience.

I'm not trying to be discouraging, just realistic. I would strongly recommend when it comes to starting out in property investment that you build your way up in complexity. Start with something quite passive and simple. Build up toward doing small renovations. Then, you can work your way up to bigger projects, rather than jumping in the deep end before you have the expertise or the knowledge.

CASE STUDY

Comparing passive property investment to refurbishments, generally the target returns or uplift in value for a refurbishment is around 10–15%, and that's after buying the right property that allows for the work to be done, doing all the work yourself, or hiring the right contractors to do it and pulling it off successfully. Many of our clients invest in off plan property, and by finding the right property in an area that is moving in the right direction, and utilising our buying power to get the right price, we generally achieve an uplift in value of 10–15% over the build period without any time from the investor required.

Comparing the two, very similar returns in the right circumstances and far less risk and time applied by the investor for passive investment. I know which looks more attractive to me.

What have you learned?

In this chapter we've discussed that it makes sense to borrow to invest in property, but is riskier to borrow for shares. We have also dealt with the benefits of borrowing, and how to calculate the investable asset base you will need to replace your income.

You learned that the returns generated from leveraged buy to let property greatly exceed the returns generated by other popular investment asset classes, and that property tends to be a more stable investment option over other investments. We have covered the two ways to buy property:

1. Debt free property

2. Leveraged property

And finally, leveraged property generally generates a stronger return, but positive cash flow property is the ideal scenario.

Questions for you

1. Do you currently have a buy to let property or portfolio and, if so, is it generating the yield that you want or need?

2. Have you calculated what investable asset base you need to replace your income?

3. Are you on track for achieving that investable asset in a timeframe that you are happy with?

4. If not, have you sought advice on how to improve your strategy?

At Nova, we recognise the importance of having goals on any investment journey, and especially when investing in property. We've developed our Property Investor's Scorecard to help everyone better understand their current situation, their goals, and to start to think about a strategy for achieving them and determine your Property IQ. You can find our Property Investor's Scorecard here: www.nova. financial/scorecard. Good luck!

Now that you understand the basics involved in buying property, the next chapter will move onto the financials. In particular you will find out about the RETIRE Investment Journey which is my six-step model to financial freedom for your retirement.

CHAPTER THREE

Understand Your Current Financial Position

When it comes to improving your financial position, firstly you must understand what you're improving on. The key areas are your:

- current income

- expenses

- net disposable income (your income minus expenses)

- current assets such as a home, personal possessions and investments

- debts

From there you will be able to determine your net asset position, which is your assets minus your debts;

and your net investable asset base, which is your investment assets minus your debts. This is your starting point. In this chapter, you will be given the tools to become clear on what personal assets and investment assets are, and importantly, what is good and bad debt and how to use good debt wisely.

We will also cover the RETIRE Investment Journey, a six-step model to help you prepare for your retirement. We will start with the difference between personal assets and investment assets, and personal debt and investment debt. We'll also look at the use of each of these and how they can positively and negatively affect your finances.

Budgeting

Budgeting is critical for any household. If you spend more than you earn, your finances will be a mess, and you'll get yourself in trouble as this is an unsustainable pattern. Whether it's a detailed budget that uses forecasting and real time expenses to calculate exactly what you can and cannot spend to the penny, or just a simple 'back of the envelope' calculation will depend on your situation and how numbers-savvy you are. One of the two, or somewhere in between, is essential when you start investing in properties, and becomes even more important once you're juggling both your own income and expenses, and that of your family.

Ideally your budget should account for your net income. Then, subtract all of your expenses including costs such as housing, groceries and travel, and allow for any potential unforeseen expenses such as doctors' bills as well as savings.

If this is the first time you have done a budget or it has been fairly ad-hoc/back of the envelope, you can go to www.nova.financial/budgetdownload for a template to work from.

Depending on your situation, try to aim for three types of expenses – housing, general expenses and savings/investment funds.

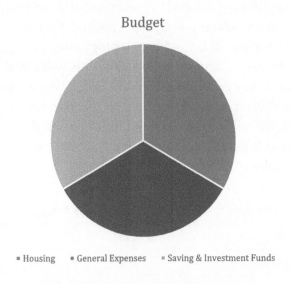

Fig 3.1 A simple budget

While this is an oversimplified example, it's a useful target for everyone to aim for. Even if your expenses utilise 40% or 50% of your net income, you will still be saving 10% to 20%. What's important is that you're saving something and improving your situation rather than living week to week. There is no point working hard just to get by. If that is where you are now, look for new ways to change it. You will need to either reduce your expenses or increase your income, or a combination of both. We now live in a world of abundance, and it's never been easier to make money. Please appreciate this and make the best use of the opportunities that are available to you. In the not too distant past, in the agricultural and industrial age, it was extremely difficult to create wealth from nothing, because to make money you needed to own farms or factories. Today with a laptop, some Googling, maybe some courses and a good attitude, you can make a very tidy living fairly quickly. There are many different types of assets but for the purpose of this book we will categorise them into two simple groups – lifestyle assets and investment assets. Here are some examples of these:

Lifestyle Assets	Investment Assets
Home	Cash
Car	Shares
Furniture	Buy to let property

Lifestyle assets make your life easier and more comfortable. They generally cost money to buy and maintain, and in many cases, they depreciate in value. For example, a car bought five years ago will generally be worth less now than what you paid for it.

Investment assets also cost money to buy, but they should generate a return in the form of income and / or capital growth. They appreciate in value or at least give a cash flow return and maintain their value, in the right circumstances. However, please note that investment assets can of course decrease in value as well. Having your dream home is a great achievement and often one major lifestyle goal for many people. But if all of your money is tied up in buying that dream home and you have a huge mortgage on it without any other assets, then it will be difficult to generate an income from your asset base unless you sell and invest or re-mortgage to release equity.

I meet far too many people in their sixties who have a multi-million-pound home but no investment assets. They have worked hard all their lives and ploughed so much money into that prized home and don't want to leave it, but also can't afford to provide for their retirement. It's a difficult situation that you don't want to end up in – so always think about building an investment asset base as well as providing yourself with life's comforts.

It's a personal decision as to how you want to allocate your resources, but if you were to ask me which is most important between personal assets and investment assets, I'd say investment assets without a doubt. This is especially true if you're young or lack investment assets: some short-term pain can and should result in long term gain. If you're dead set on buying that car you've always wanted, then invest first in appreciating assets and make the money or the cash flow to fund it rather than spending all of your money on a depreciating asset.

As with assets, there are also two types of debt – good debt and bad debt. Good debt is investment debt which is generally tax deductible. If used prudently it allows you to improve your financial position and to better utilise your money. We will go into much more detail on property investment debt later, but for now the point is that the prudent use of investment debt (good debt) can allow you to achieve your goals a lot sooner. It also has the ability to allow those with limited resources to achieve a lot more than they would without it.

Bad debt is lifestyle debt which is generally used for the purpose of buying a house, a car, an expensive handbag or a holiday, for example. It improves your quality of life initially, but costs you a lot more than investment debt as it rarely helps improve your finances and can often damage them. We live in a society that craves instant satisfaction through credit cards and other lifestyle debts. In a presentation by The Money Charity entitled 'The Money Statistics', the average UK household had a record high £12,887 of unsecured debt and £20,908 was spent every second on debit and credit cards in 2017.[14] Including mortgages, the average person owed £56,000 or 113% of their income, and 248 people were made bankrupt each day. Watching your budget and accumulating debt only for the right reasons is crucial.

I understand the reluctance some people have with regards to debt. Many people who are considering investing have spent a good portion of their lives trying to pay down their home loan, so why would they now take on more debt? The answer is that without debt it's very difficult to achieve your goals unless you are earning a lot of money already and can funnel that money into investments. If this is a concern of yours, I encourage you to separate good debt from bad debt in your mind. Think about the prudent use of investment debt as a good thing, and lifestyle debt as a bad thing. Don't get stressed about having good debt, but be proud that you have been smart enough to use someone else's money to make you money.

The RETIRE Investment Journey

With a better understanding of your financial situation and a clear idea of your budget, you can now begin to

---

14 The Money Statistics, February 2017. The Money Charity

take the necessary steps to plan a retirement in which you are financially free. I have developed the RETIRE Investment Journey firstly because I thought it was a nifty little acronym which makes it easy to remember, and secondly because it clearly defines the journey towards a comfortable retirement from start to finish.

There are six steps in the RETIRE Investment Journey:

1. Ready to get started

2. Education

3. Testing the water

4. Investing further

5. Retirement transitioning

6. Easy retirement

Completing each stage will enable you to create an asset base that builds your wealth and helps you achieve the ultimate goal of financial freedom, a comfortable retirement or the ability to retire whenever you want. You define your end goal. Let's take a run through each stage in more detail.

Ready to get started

At this stage of your life you're just starting to think about investing. For most people this is between the ages of twenty-five and thirty-five, but don't worry if you're outside this bracket, as many successful people started earlier or later than this. This is the beginning of financial awareness, and it's the time when you realise that working longer hours to earn more money but then spending it all on a more expensive lifestyle is not enough. You want to learn how to use your money better. Congratulations! This is the first step in a long but essential process towards achieving financial freedom. Now you must utilise all resources available to you to achieve awareness and take action. Be acutely aware that without action, nothing changes!

Education

In this stage, research and education is of the utmost importance. You need to build your knowledge base, your network, and ideally seek the guidance of a trusted advisor to assist you to get started on the right path. This is essentially the cornerstone of your investment journey, as often the first investment will either give you the confidence to keep going or you will get your fingers burnt which could affect your progress.

Do your research but try not to self-diagnose. This is comparable to going online and looking up why you have a sore throat. Often you will end up thinking you have a life-threatening disease when in fact you just have a cold. Seeking advice on what is right for your situation and what you are trying to achieve is akin to going to the doctor. This doesn't mean that you shouldn't do your own research, but there is a lot of conflicting information out there that can often result in paralysis by analysis. You can spend far too much time going around in circles – remember that until you have invested you have not actually achieved anything with regards to improving your financial situation, so don't spend too much time on this stage as you can learn on the go. Jumping in the deep end and learning to swim can be a good option with the right guidance, especially if you have a proclivity to procrastinate.

Testing the water

Starting with a low risk investment where you're very confident on steady returns is advisable at this stage. All too often I see first time investors trying to be too creative to create 'fast equity' which they have heard about at a get rich quick seminar. Such investments are often high risk and profess unachievable returns, or in some cases are just non-existent solely for the purpose of selling a seminar. Some of the following clichés here that really ring true are:

- If it's too good to be true, then it probably is

- Where there's smoke, there's probably fire

- If it looks like a duck and quacks like a duck, it is probably a duck regardless of what a salesperson tells you it is

Don't believe the hype and use common sense at this stage of the process. My advice is to start small and with low risk, and build from there as your confidence and wealth builds and your ability to weather a loss builds also.

Investing further

At this stage, you've already made your first investment and you're now looking to build an asset base and move closer towards your long term goal. You may start to make larger investments or take on more creative projects as your confidence and wealth builds. Don't get carried away and start to think that you are an expert (unless you are). An over-confident investor is often an unwise investor, so don't jump into things unaware. Keep in mind the old saying: 'Quite often the best deals you'll do are the ones you don't do!'

Maintain in-depth research and due diligence at every turn to ensure you don't get burnt or make the wrong decision for your situation. This phase should focus on capital growth investments unless you already have a substantial investable asset base. While income is important to support costs, when you're building an asset base you're much more likely to reach your goal sooner through growth then through income.

Your investments should be chosen according to, and are dependent on, the type of return that is most

51

suitable for your stage of the investment journey. At this stage an advisor or advisory company can add a lot of value by providing the resources you need such as time, knowledge and experience. You can use them as an independent third party to help you remove emotion from your decision-making process, and focus on and amend your strategy when suitable.

Retirement transitioning

This phase is when you have reached the required asset base to generate the income that you need to live comfortably. If you haven't done so already then go back to the previous chapter and use the equation provided to calculate this for yourself. Often the investments you have made while building an asset base have been capital growth focused and may not be generating sufficient income for you. This is a common shift to which there are a few solutions. For example, you could sell up and completely shift into income focused investments, or you could liquidate part of your portfolio or choose to re-mortgage to release equity to accommodate the shift towards strong income generating assets.

The answer will differ depending on your situation, but it's important to remain commercially minded and not get attached to investments regardless of how well they have performed if they're not generating the right type of income for you. It's crucial at this phase to seek advice as the option you ultimately choose could have a massive impact on the outcome for you in retirement.

A family friend of mine recently inherited a reasonable sum and invested in ten small factories in a regional town of the UK. Aside from being slightly offended that he didn't ask me for investment advice on what he should do with the money, I thought he was crazy. What could ten factories in a small town have going for them as an investment? They're never going to grow in value and surely there is not that much demand from tenants, or so I thought. I asked him why he did it, and his response was that he had pre-leased them for twenty years at a 10% plus yield, and given that he is sixty years of age, he couldn't care less about growth as the kids could worry about that. Little did I know that my family friend clearly understood that he had the asset base required to generate the income that he needed and wasn't worried about the exit strategy or growth, as it will be beyond his timeframe of caring. Not so crazy!

Easy retirement

If the previous phases have been done right to best utilise your resources and achieve the income that you need, then this phase is about enjoying the fruits of your labour. Whatever your goals were, they should now be achieved and you're able to enjoy life and appreciate the work that you put into getting you here. Now of course you may need to tweak things here and there based on economic or legislative changes, but ideally they can be looked after by someone else.

CASE STUDY

John's end goal is £50,000 per annum, but at this stage he only has £50,000 to invest.

A £50,000 investment into a 10% NET yielding asset (the upper end of what is achievable today) will give John £5,000 per annum. This means that if the asset that John invested in doesn't grow in value, then £5,000 is all he will ever get in a year. To achieve his £50,000 per annum, he would therefore need to save nine more lots of £50,000 to achieve his income goal of £50,000 per annum. This is going to be very difficult, if even possible at all, for most people given current average income per annum of circa £26,000.

The same £50,000 invested into a £200,000 property with 75% leverage that doubles in value over ten to fifteen years (about what the UK property has done over the past few decades) means that the £50,000 John invested is then worth £250,000 (£400,000 property with £150,000 of debt). If John does that four times over by applying some further funds and perhaps re-mortgaging every few years to release equity, he will have turned his £50,000 into £1,000,000. This may seem farfetched, but in fact it's very achievable over a circa twenty-year time frame, which means if you start between the age of thirty to forty you should be able to achieve this between fifty and sixty, which are about the average ages people start thinking about investing and then want to retire.

John will be much more likely to achieve the income he wants in the subsequent phases of his investment journey: a 5% yield on £1,000 000 is £50,000 which is his income goal. This can be likened to growing and squeezing an orange: when you have a small orange, there's not much point in picking and squeezing it because you're unlikely to get much juice. When that orange has grown big and juicy, that is the time to squeeze. The orange is your asset base and the juice is your cash flow.

What have you learned?

There are two types of assets – personal and investment. Personal assets improve your short-term lifestyle but are often depreciating. Investment assets improve your finances and are often appreciating.

There are also two types of debt – good and bad. Learn how to use good debt to build your wealth. There are six stages to the RETIRE Investment Journey, all of which, when acted upon, will help you build your asset base and your wealth.

Questions for you

1. What is your monthly savings capacity? Make sure to go to www.nova.financial/budgetdownload to access the tool to help you work this out.

2. Where are you in the RETIRE Investment Journey?

3. Have you sought professional advice on how you could improve your strategy?

4. How can you use the RETIRE Investment Journey model to start to plan your financially free retirement?

Go to the Property Investor's Scorecard on our website to assess your current situation and determine your Property IQ: www.nova.financial/scorecard

A crucial factor to successful investment is to get an understanding of your appetite for risk. All types of investment involve taking some risk. Once you understand your tolerance level you can then set goals that are realistic and achievable and will keep you focused on your road to successful investment.

UNDERSTANDING PROPERTY

In this next section – understanding property – you will learn about the ten fundamentals, the passive investment, how to finance your properties and get a clear understanding of structuring rules affecting property investment and making sure you stick to them.

There are key mistakes I see made by people starting out on their investment journey who haven't done their research. They've simply jumped in when they see what they think is a good deal, only to find that they regret their investment further down the line.

Why property? The first thing we will look at in this section is why you should invest in property: and that comes down to the ability to leverage and generate strong returns on the cash invested with confidence, even if the returns on the asset are relatively average. The risk return balance of leveraged property, in my view, is better than any other investment option because when you combine capital growth and cash flow returns on the funds invested, 30% plus returns per annum is very achievable. That is because you have essentially quadrupled your money using leverage, which compounds the return.

By investing in the right properties in the right areas that are going to rent every day of the year due to desirability factors, and that we think will grow in value due to supply outweighing demand, we can be confident of actually achieving that return without taking too much risk. Then it comes down to finding the right properties and I will give you a framework to help you find the right properties in the right locations.

CHAPTER FOUR

Set Your Goals

On his website, Tony Robbins says, 'Setting goals is the first step to turning the invisible into the visible'. It stands to reason that you must first know what your goals are and the timeframes in which you would like to achieve them before trying to figure out how to get there. That sounds obvious, right? It can't be that obvious, as many people start making investments 'willy nilly' and without any real direction. No two people's situations are exactly the same, and often their goals and timeframes for achieving them will be different. Having clearly defined and written down goals is the first step to achieving them. But before you get started there are some key issues to consider.

1. Your risk profile

What is your appetite for risk? All investments have an element of risk and return. If you don't want to take any risk, then put your money in the bank and receive a very minimal return. But most experienced investors and advisors will tell you that doing so is an under-utilisation of your funds, and that you can take a measured approach to risk to achieve a much better return. If you're not sure what your risk tolerance is, but you know you don't want to take too much risk, then you're in luck! The principles in this book focus on passive property investments in areas which are relatively stable and therefore low risk. A quick do-it-yourself test to determine whether you have the stomach for borrowing to invest in shares is the following:

If you saw the value of your life savings fall by 50% or more in a matter of days and the lender wanted you to sell or put in more money, what would you do?

a. Sell all your investments

b. Sell part of your investment to cover the margin call

c. Put in more money

If your answer is a or b, then borrowing to invest in shares probably isn't your thing, as you would have sold at the worst possible time. If you feel more comfortable investing for the long term, with leverage but without the risk of margin calls and without being able to check the exact value of your investment every day, then property is probably best for you. A trusted advisor can give you a much clearer understanding of your risk profile and what works best for you, your situation and your preferences.

2. Have a clear strategy

Inherently as human beings, we tend to go about life in a rather ad-hoc fashion given our busy lives with family and work. But the issue with 'floating' through life is that we don't have any clear direction. This is especially evident when it comes to investing with the aim of achieving specific end goals. We've already discussed clearly defining goals and understanding what it is that we are working towards, and now it's important to reverse engineer that to determine the best way of getting there.

Rather than just investing every now and again when you come into a lump sum of money or are able to save a pot of funds, actually understanding what particular investments are right for you and the correct way to structure them can make a huge difference. Of course, you could jump on Zoopla or Rightmove or any property portal and see a property you like, buy it and hope for the best – but is that likely to deliver the best possible outcomes when compared to a considered strategic approach? Not likely.

3. Understand the type of return that is right for you

When it comes to investing, not just in property but all types of investments, there are two main types of returns: cash flow and capital growth. Cash flow is the income generated by the investment and capital growth is the increase in value. It's very important to understand what type of return works best for you when considering your stage of life and your goals. In a general sense, capital growth is most important when building an asset base, and cash flow is used to support the debt with maybe a bit left over for flexibility. Once you've built the asset base that you need, cash flow becomes important to generate the income you require. It's important not to turn to cash flow until you have an acceptable size asset base as it's going to be very difficult to generate a decent cash flow unless you're sure you have the right strategy for your stage of life and financial position.

How to set your goals

Having a strategy is essential to generating the income you require, and setting the right goals to achieve that strategy is crucial. Without a goal you will go about your investment journey in a very ad-hoc way. But with a goal in mind you will have direction for everything you do. Rather than having a scattergun approach and buying properties here and there and hoping for the best, you will take a strategic approach to each investment and only make the decision to buy if it helps you achieve your goal.

We help our clients to take a more strategic approach to property investment and work towards their end lifestyle and financial goals. This way, our clients make better, more informed decisions that prevent them aimlessly buying property that may not fit with their best strategy or help them achieve their goals. When working with our clients, we take them through several key steps to help them understand their situation, define and develop their goals and then put in place a strategy for achieving them. We start with understanding the passive income they are going to need in the future and when they want to have it, as we discussed in the previous chapter. And usually that end goal is about replacing their employment income. Most people never think about this. They don't think about the end goal.

The next step is to calculate the investable asset base amount that we are actually working towards. Once the client knows that amount, they can take the final step and work out their strategy for getting there.

By putting these steps into action, a client identifies they have £100,000 net assets now and they want £1,000,000 in twenty years' time. Their shortfall is £900,000. Using our Property Investor's Scorecard or the equation in the previous chapter, the client knows they're going to have to accumulate £45,000 every year to reach their goal. Armed with this information they can work out how often they can buy another property and what net yield that property will give them, and the expected growth and return on that property. Once they have that information, they can work out how aggressive they need to be in saving, re-mortgaging and re-investing and plan their strategy to reach their end goal.

If, in planning your goal, you find you have to take steps that might hurt your lifestyle then it's important to be aware of this. One way of being more aggressive could be that you have to save a bigger portion of your income or not spend large sums on holidays, or you might have to invest in slightly more risky assets or re-mortgage to re-invest more often. Think about how much money you need on a yearly basis to live comfortably – for example, £50,000 yearly – and to achieve £50,000 on a 5% net return you will require £1,000,000 in investable assets. Investable assets are defined as your net worth; the value of the assets minus the liability, while excluding your home since it doesn't generate you an income. Ideally you would like the income to be generated passively and not from having to work five to six days a week. This is what we call passive income. You can achieve more, but generally a 5% return is very achievable regardless of the state of the economy.

If numbers aren't your forte then a simpler way of working it out (other than our Property Investor's

Scorecard) is to take whatever your required yearly figure is, then double it and add a zero, and that should be your long term goal for investable assets:

$$£50k \times 2 = £100k, \text{ with zero added} = £1M$$

Your investable asset base target may seem daunting, but at least we now know what we're working towards and perhaps that will build some urgency into you doing something about it.

Now think about when you would like to realistically achieve the passive income you need, and that gives you your timeframe.

Divide what you want by what you need to save each month. For example, £1,000,000 is your required asset base to generate £50,000 of passive income. You would like to achieve this goal in twenty years, so £1,000,000 divided by twenty (the number of years to achieve your goal) divided by twelve (the number of months in years) equals £2,777 a month.

For most that would seem absolutely impossible as many people do not earn that much a month before, let alone after, tax. I would hope that by this stage of the book you've realised that the way to achieve it is through investing. If you invest £100 a month at an 8% per annum return over thirty years you will have £186,253 or at £200 a month you would get to £393,476!

Should you invest now or wait a while? A very relevant Chinese proverb says: 'The best time to plant a tree is twenty years ago and the second-best time is now.' We can't go back twenty years to plant a tree, but investment success is a function of time and smart decisions. Don't try to pick the market or wait for the perfect time to improve your financial position and invest. Get started now to give yourself the best chance of achieving your goals. This is where having an Investors Mindset comes into play, which we will be talking about next. In my opinion, especially with property investment, it's about *time in the market* rather than *timing the market*. Invest wisely as soon as possible and ride the investment cycle to success.

The Investor Mindset

If possible, when it comes to investing, you should be completely commercially minded and remove all emotions. The 'if possible' is a big caveat, since everyone is, to some extent, emotional in their decision-making process whether they like to admit it or not. Both who we are and our personalities are products of our environment and our experiences, so of course our decision-making process is going to be impacted by those past experiences and preconceptions.

Start by treating a property that you would potentially invest in as completely different to a home you would buy. A common attitude I hear is

'I wouldn't invest in a property that I wouldn't live in myself' but what if you live in a four-bedroom house and the best investment in a certain location that works for you is a one-bedroom apartment? You probably wouldn't want to live there, but it could be the perfect property for a young professional. It's not so much about what you want or like, but what the target market wants and likes that will determine the investment outcome.

Separate your own preferences when selecting investments and get to know your target market well. If you do have preconceptions about a type of property or location, then make sure they are based on solid facts and not what someone said or what you might have read once. Make informed and logical choices based on research and trusted advice. But more importantly, the Investor Mindset is about taking action. Without action you will never achieve your goals.

So, here are my top tips for setting the goals and strategy for successful passive property investment:

1. Determine your risk profile

2. Understand your current situation, and define your goals and timeframes for achieving them

3. Reverse engineer your goals and timeframes into a strategy for achieving them

4. Be unemotional and commercially minded in selecting the right property investments for you

5. TAKE ACTION!

CASE STUDY

There was a survey of Harvard MBA students in 1985 where the students were asked if they had clearly defined and written down goals and a plan for achieving them. The results suggested were:

- 3% said that they did
- 13% percent said they had goals but they were not written down
- The rest (84%) said they didn't

They apparently surveyed that same group ten years later and the first group, the 3%, were earning ten times as much as the other 97% combined.

Unfortunately, there is no evidence that the study was actually done, but you will find lots of information about it by Googling it. Let's imagine that in this instance it's true and that just by writing down your goals you could earn ten times more than those who didn't. How would that change your strategy to property investment? True or not, what this story tells us is that it's important to have clearly defined and written down goals and if we do then we are far more likely to achieve them.

What have you learned?

Setting goals will give you direction in making property investments and building a portfolio. Having a strategy to achieve that goal will stop you having a scattergun approach to buying properties. To set your goal you need to:

- Know what passive income you want to achieve and by when

- Calculate the investable amount you're actually working towards

- Plan your strategy for getting there

Questions for you

1. What is your attitude to risk?

2. What was your answer to whether you have the stomach for borrowing to invest in shares?

3. Do you see the benefits to borrowing to invest in property?

4. Given your answers to these questions, is property investment the right investment strategy for you?

Go to the Property Investor's Scorecard on our website and work through the steps to set your goals and plan your strategy for achieving them, and determine your Property IQ: www.nova.financial/scorecard

In the next chapter you will learn about my Ten Fundamentals to Successful Property Investment. Once you have a clear understanding of these principles you'll find it easier to buy properties that you can keep rented and bring you the return on investment you want.

CHAPTER FIVE

Property Research, Due Diligence And Sourcing

Property investment is a vehicle to achieving a financial goal in the future, especially when using leverage (mortgages). It's the most suitable investment asset for the broadest range of people. Investing, however, is not just about what makes sense on a spreadsheet. It's also about what gives you peace of mind. If you can't sleep at night because of an investment you've made, then it's simply not the right one for you.

There are ten fundamentals to successful passive property investment:

1. Supply

2. Demand

3. Target market

4. Location

5. Infrastructure

6. Price

7. Fair Value

8. Economic changes and legislation

9. Vendors

10. Type of property

In this chapter I will provide an overview of each for you to use as you start your investment journey, or as a refresher for those with experience.

Supply

Supply is the availability of property in an area, and includes current supply and the likelihood of future supply. Areas where there is a lack of current supply and a lack of ability for future supply are ideal since this creates supply tension and drives up prices. This is most prevalent in areas where land is a limited commodity. In major cities are, for example, employment and infrastructure hubs with strong demand, but only so much can be built at a time.

This imbalance between supply and demand is what drives both rental and price growth.

CASE STUDY

In the UK, pretty much every major city is undersupplied with property. The UK government recently stated that there is a requirement for 300,000 new properties per annum to meet demand and the average for the past 10 years has been around 150,000, so only half of what is required. While you have statistics like that in a market, it is impossible to argue against prices increasing over the mid to long term.

The Manchester City Council (MCC) recently announced that there is a requirement for 5,000 new properties per annum in the metropolitan area, that there is a backlog of 40,000 and the average for the past five years has been 1,500. This can't change overnight and has resulted in very strong property price growth in Manchester over recent years. At the time of writing in 2018, there is currently circa 13,000 units planned for delivery in Manchester over the next four years which in isolation seems like a lot, but according to the MCC it's still 7,000 short of what is required (not considering the backlog).

Demand

Demand is the combination of people currently living in an area, and future population growth which increases demand. Population growth is the combination of immigration and net migration (people moving between cities within a country) within the country. Demand and growth are driven by the availability of a broad range of industries, employment, infrastructure, facilities and amenities which results in a large tenant pool and strong demand. Strong demand reduces vacancy rates and ensures that you always have a tenant – and constant income from your investment.

Demand is often driven by desirability. If you have a desirable property in a desirable area, then there should always be demand. Of course, it will need to be balanced with price. If investing in the right area, demand can reduce the risk of an economic downturn in the rental market. The price of your property may fall, but as long as you're not selling at that time it doesn't really matter since markets are cyclical and the price should bounce back. The rental demand and income will continue strongly in an economic downturn, or even increase, due to less mortgage funding available and more rental pressure in areas with strong employment.

Target market

Who do you plan to rent your property to, and eventually sell to, in the future? Young professionals, social housing and/or families? Young professionals often earn above average incomes and are willing to pay more for a nice place in a nice area. Young professionals are the ideal target market. Social housing tenants tend to live in cheaper properties in cheaper areas. Cheaper properties can provide great yields and a steady income, as the local authority pays the tenants rent. However, these tenants can be short on funds and could divert money paid to them for your rental payment towards other expenses. Since they aren't responsible for their deposit, they may not have as much respect for the property.

Family tenants are a good long term target market as they tend to stay in the same property longer than young professionals. They typically have a more stable source of income than social housing tenants. To target families, you need to consider infrastructure, schools and vacancy rates. These are the factors that drive demand. Understand what your target market wants. If single occupancy rates or one-person households in an area are very high, then a one-bedroom apartment is a sensible investment. If it's a family area, then a three-bedroom house is good. Many people go wrong by investing in a one bed in the family area because it's cheaper than a city centre. But if there's no demand for that property then vacancy rates will be higher and resale may be difficult. It's important that you invest in an area with strong demand that is skewed towards the type of property you are buying. Understanding the statistics is important for understanding your target market in certain locations. The Office of National Statistics (www.ons.gov.uk) is very useful.

Location

Invest in locations with as much depth as possible. These are areas that are stable and reliable. By depth, I mean large tenant pools and strong tenant demand, a broad range of industries, and high and diverse employment. You'll get this diversity in major cities, whereas smaller cities and towns are often driven by one industry or even one employer. If they fail, so too does your target market and your demand. For example, if you invested in Sheffield in the 1970s your investment was directly impacted by the steel industry. When the steel industry went under, so too would have your investment. Making sure you have that diversity gives peace of mind in stability.

The terms 'blue chip' and 'speculative' can be applied to property. Blue chip are big stable investments, and speculative are volatile, small, and less reliable investments. A blue chip, stable investment would be one close to city areas or city collar towns. The farther you are from a city, the more your risk increases, and your investment becomes more speculative because the depth thins. You can achieve fantastic performance in these speculative areas, and there is generally great hype about the next 'fad' area to invest in, where a relatively small amount of money flowing into these areas can cause a boom. However, booms can turn to bust and a lack of interest or reduced investment can cause a crash or the market to stagnate.

We prefer steady, reliable investments for our clients, and this is achieved in blue chip city surrounding areas. At the time of writing in 2018, in the UK, the central locations and surrounding areas in London, Manchester, Birmingham, Liverpool and Leeds have all of the components necessary for good property investment. In a recession, rents in these city locations can often increase due to the availability of finance decreasing and increase in rental pressure. Jobs also dry up in regional locations so people flock to the major cities for work. Young professionals want to live around city centres that feature strong employment, facilities, amenities and infrastructure such as public transport, pubs, restaurants, bars and cafés.

Property prices and rents won't just grow in value for no reason. There needs to be a growth-driving factor, which is generally a lack of supply versus demand. If you invest in an area where not much changes, then you're unlikely to achieve growth. Consider the socio-economic levels and demographics of an area such as average incomes, vacancy rates, employment rates and average ages. The Office for National Statistics is a good source of this information.

Once you've done your research you can then decide whether to invest in areas with strong incomes, low unemployment and room for growth. Or perhaps you've identified a catalyst for change that will cause a gentrification of an area where the stats are not currently the best, but should improve. One example of a catalyst for change is major infrastructure projects.

About 90% of people invest within five miles of their own homes. At first glance this makes sense, as they can manage the property easily. However, what are the chances of the best investment being within five miles of your own home when, for example, there are 243,610 square miles in the UK? When investing, we need to be commercially minded – the goal is to make money. With a good property manager, your property can be anywhere, and if there are better investments further away then you should utilise them.

Infrastructure

Infrastructure is essential if your chosen investment area is going to be desirable to your target market. Large infrastructure includes roads and rail, whereas small includes bars, restaurants and cafés. Highways and railways transform a location.

CASE STUDY

A perfect example is the Crossrail in London, which at the time of writing is still about two years from being completed, but many areas have already experienced price growth of 50% plus which is strongly attributed to this future utility. There will be more growth when it's completed and the utility is in place.

As travel times from towns on the outskirts into Central London are cut, the commuter belt increases. According to Stefanie Garber in her article, 'Will Crossrail drive up house prices?' if you invested in an average property in Woolwich, south east London seven years ago, your property would be worth 85% more today, largely due to Crossrail speculation resulting in gentrification of that area.[15]

Another example is Hackney, which is the fastest growing town in the UK over the past thirty years with growth of 800%. Twenty years ago, Hackney was a low socio-economic area five miles from Central London. It was a crime hub and properties were cheap, however it benefited from the ripple effect that London provided. As London became more expensive, those that could no longer afford to live centrally or wanted more space were pushed further out.[16] Added

---

15 Garber, S. 'Will Crossrail drive up house prices?' *Which News*, 9 September 2018

16 Pettitt, J. 'East end property boom sees Hackney house prices rise 800 percent in under 30 years', 2014, www.standard.co.uk/news/london/east-end-property-boom-outstripped-chelsea-and-westminster-since-1987-survey-finds-9710564.html

to this was the improvement in the tube line and a hipster renaissance. Put these together and you have a booming Hackney property market.

Regeneration of an area creates new facilities and amenities, such as new build residential and commercial developments, conversion of existing buildings, shopping centres and schools. Each of these facilities attract new people and makes restaurants, bars and cafés more viable due to footfall. A perfect example of regeneration and gentrification is the town of Hackney in east London.

Development is driven by confidence and new construction, and regeneration has the potential to improve the live-ability of an area and drive further demand. New shopping centres, cafés and commercial space which improve employment often impact residential property prices in a positive way. When you see inward investment into an area, such as a new Waitrose or Tesco, it's rarely a bad sign. These companies don't spend large sums of money on a whim. They, and foreign direct investment, are commonly driven by growing confidence in an area.

Price

Value is important when it comes to property investment. However, surveyors determine their valuations based upon comparable sales in the area and good old-fashioned guess work. Websites such as Zoopla and Rightmove provide quick and easy valuation services but they are often inaccurate, especially if there hasn't been many comparable sales of similar property in that area. A brand new property with top of the range fixtures and fittings is not comparable to a 100-year-old property on the other side of town. Searching lowest to highest on Zoopla is a terrible idea, as you will first be presented with the cheapest and nastiest properties in an area.

Balance price with desirability. Cheap properties are cheap for a reason: there's usually a lack of demand driven by a lack of desirability. An undesirable property will not rent or sell well which is really the opposite of what you want in a good investment. If you're an experienced builder or fancy yourself as a 'Homes under the Hammer' contestant, then of course you could do a major renovation. But renovation should not be considered the easy road to riches. Many investors have been burnt by dodgy-Dave builders and estate agents that over-promise and under-deliver. Buyer beware.

When I'm looking for a new property, I target areas with strong rental yields, affordable property prices relative to average incomes, strong employment and employment growth, and existing infrastructure as well as future infrastructure planned or underway. Essentially, these are all the ingredients that equate to a market moving in the right direction.

Fair value

Pay fair value for the right property in an upward market. Many people focus on getting the 'deal' price or a distressed sale, but remember that you want a desirable property in a desirable location where there is strong demand. If you're buying a property where others see the potential and therefore demand is strong, the price is not going to be low. But that doesn't mean it will not perform well as an investment. In fact, properties where you begrudgingly pay a bit more than you expected quite often perform better due to the market determining that they're a good buy. All too often I speak with people that thought they got a 'deal' but in fact they bought a lemon.

Watch out for unscrupulous property salespeople selling property at Below Market Value (BMV). Often these valuations are overestimated. You can, of course, buy at a very good value or at the right price in certain circumstances like forced sellers, foreclosures or in a depressed market. But don't assume it to be the case just because it seems 'cheap'. Buying at the right value is obviously what we want to be doing, but certainly don't be sucked in by the buzz word of BMV.

Economic changes & legislation

Consider the current and potential future changes to the economy and legislation when investing. This chapter will cover three different issues – the economy, the property cycle and tax changes. Let's take each in turn.

1. **The economy**

   The economic cycle impacts property in ways such as availability of finance, interest rates, property supply, population growth, job availability, number of buyers in the market and confidence. Prices won't move exactly in alignment with the economic cycle but they will be affected. As discussed earlier, it's very important to buy properties in locations with depth which will make it easier to survive downturns as you're still likely to have a tenant paying you rent.

2. **The property cycle**

   The length of the property cycle and where we are on it at any one time causes much debate, but there is undoubtedly a cycle. The most commonly accepted property cycle of eighteen years was first published by Fred Harrison in *'Boom and Bust'* in 2005. He predicted the 2007/08 downturn with uncanny accuracy, identifying a four-year downturn followed by seven years of moderate growth, and then seven years of strong growth with a mid-cycle wobble in between. This corresponds with the UK property market with moderate price rises since 2011/2012, the mid-term wobble of late 2017/2018, which according to Harrison would be followed by strong growth through to 2025 before another pull back in values (or a crash, as some would call it but I prefer the term downturn as the property market rarely falls enough to justify the word crash) at the end of the cycle. According to Harrison, this cycle has been playing out for the past 100 years.

3. Tax changes

In 2015 and 2016 there were a range of tax changes announced which made property investments with mortgages less tax efficient. Once implemented they technically made mortgage interest no longer tax deductible, but instead a tax credit would be given after the calculation of net income on which the tax was payable. Further, a Stamp Duty premium was introduced for any subsequent property purchase (other than your first) of 3% on top of the current thresholds. This, however, is not the end for property investment, as there are ways that you can deal with this and certain properties which are more affected then others, and we will discuss this further in a later chapter.

Vendors

If buying a new build or an off plan property, check the developer's track record. Do they deliver on time and a quality product? What have they done in the past? Have previous buyers been happy with them? Look at their financial statements and determine their financial strength. Do your research and your due diligence. Bring in an expert advisor to help you who understands the market and the best vendors to work with. Get as much information as you can, and make an informed decision on whether you are buying from the right people and whether they will deliver on their promises.

This becomes important when you are buying new property and especially off plan property, where the asset that you are buying is not necessarily in existence yet. There is a level of faith and commercially minded decision-making required to give you the confidence to make that purchase.

It is also a good idea for your deposit to be protected in some way in case of developer insolvency. There are different ways to achieve this and you should seek advice. I also recommend against buying off plan properties where the deposit is more than 35% as the funds you're applying are often at risk. Deposits of 10% are standard in London, and outside London where properties are cheaper they're generally 20-30%. Any more than that and your funds are often being used to fund the development and that can end badly if something goes wrong.

Type of property

There are several factors to consider here:

1. Houses versus apartments

2. New off plan or second hand

3. Land component

4. Size of development

I'll give you an overview of each in turn:

1. Houses versus apartments.

As covered in previous chapters, we prefer to invest, and have our clients invest, in central locations with depth. In city centre locations, apartments tend to be the more suitable type of property particularly for young professionals. Houses are good in family-oriented areas, but the type of property should be determined by what the target market wants.

The determining factor should have nothing to do with your personal preferences or beliefs. Remember, we are commercially minded investors and property is the vehicle for achieving financial freedom. You need to first determine the right area to invest in, then choose the right type of property in that area.

There are three other important factors to take account of. Firstly, whether you should consider a new build, off plan property or a second hand home. Secondly, whether you should buy a property with a land component included and thirdly, the size of development should you buy in.

2. New build versus second hand.

New properties come with a range of warranties, such as a two-year builder's defect period which covers all minor defects for that period and a ten-year structural warranty which covers design defects, structural issues and water ingress. Furthermore, the fixtures and fittings tend to be under warranty for five to seven years. New build properties are low maintenance properties where you can have confidence in costs and net returns. They also often come with all the latest 'bells and whistles' which attract the top end of the rental market. Given that we view property as a box that generates money, very unemotionally and commercially minded, we want low maintenance projects and to have confidence in what our costs are. New build property does that.

With older properties, you may have to spend money on them but you won't know what that money is yet. I want you to be an investor rather than a landlord fixing toilets on the weekends. Sorry to those that consider themselves 'landlords', but our goal is to make money. The last thing you want is a money pit for an investment. A great example of this are Victorian properties which look great, and landlords often buy them because they fall in love. However they require a lot of maintenance and are akin to buying a vintage car, every time you take it for a spin something needs replacing!

Off plan in the right circumstances can also be a great option for the passive investor. The main reasons are that you get all the passive benefits of new property but you get in first which often means you are able to purchase the best within a development, often at a very good price, and therefore position yourself for growth. We've had many clients who have achieved substantial uplifts in value just over the build period, in some cases up to a 50% uplift, as you are buying a property at today's price in tomorrow's market.

3. Land component

Having a land component in central locations or city collar towns is reliant on the area, generally quite expensive, and in most cases prohibitive to property investors' overall investment portfolio. To get a component of land you would need to look much further from city areas, unless you're looking to spend big money on one investment, which is not what we usually recommend. Consider the trend towards the repopulation of cities and city fringes and apartment living these days. Demographers call it 'space for place', as people choose to swap size for amenity and affordability. Land doesn't drive growth when investing in real estate. Property is driven by supply and demand so you must invest in what your target market desires. A great example of this is Manchester city centre; twenty years ago there were just 1,000 people living there, and now there are nearly 30,000. The old cliché of wanting a quarter acre block with a garden and a picket fence is no longer the dream of the younger generations. They want to live centrally with amenities, so if that's your target market then invest accordingly.

4. Size of development

Developers generally don't build small developments in central locations because of the cost of land and construction. You must go further from a city and incur all the risks we have discussed previously if you want a small boutique development, or often pay a higher price. However, consider that whether you are buying in a development of three or three thousand units, you're not just competing against the properties in your development, but the greater market. Bigger developments can work just as well as small, or in some cases even better, where demand is strong.

We like to buy and for our clients to purchase brand new property for the passivity that they provide, and because the investment timeframe is generally seven to fifteen years, when it comes times to sell, the property will need less renovation and a seven-to-fifteen-year-old property is still quite new and desirable. We like to buy in landmark developments with high quality fixtures and fittings and amenities on site that will attract owner occupiers in the resale market. While investors get most new developments off the ground, owner occupiers drive growth in resale four to six years down the track. Owner occupiers pay premiums to buy what they really like (as they are emotional buyers) and they ensure the properties are maintained. They select quality developments with facilities and a fantastic location, and are around half the resale market – so you want to appeal to them.

Working with these ten fundamentals when investing in property will ensure that you invest in the property that is passive and will help you reach your financial goal and give you peace of mind.

CASE STUDY

When talking with people about property investment advice we often receive wise-crack responses such as 'property investment is easy' or 'how hard is it, you buy a property, rent it and wait for prices to increase' and similar statements. Hopefully from reading this chapter you've gained a better understanding of the key fundamentals to apply when selecting locations and actual properties, and will be able to remove the 'luck' aspect and guess work.

Of late many of our clients have been investing in the Midlands and the North West of the UK, and more specifically the major cities of those regions like Manchester, Birmingham and Liverpool. Going back four or five years when we first started investing and advising clients to invest there rather than investing in London, some people called us mad. These places weren't as substantial as London and suffered after the 2007 financial crisis. Since then, each of these cities have gone from strength to strength with some of our clients achieving over a 50% uplift in value over that period, and yields of 6%+. Much greater than many London properties.

What have you learned?

1. Supply and demand are the key factors that drive rental and price growth

2. You have to invest in property that your target market wants, not what you want if you are going to make a profit

3. The ten fundamentals listed above will help you secure a successful passive property investment

Questions for you

1. Why do we prefer new build property?

2. What types of property do you have or have you been looking at, and do they fit the ten fundamentals covered in this chapter?

3. How can you use the ten fundamentals when you're buying your next property?

Please do try our Property Investor Scorecard and determine your Property IQ at: www.nova.financial/scorecard

Hopefully you've found the ten fundamentals to successful passive property investment useful, and you're on your way to making your first purchase. Now you will need to work out how to finance your investments. In the next chapter we will look at the types of mortgages available to you and how to access the right expertise to help you make the best decisions.

SECTION THREE

UNDERSTANDING IMPLEMENTATION

Everything we've looked at in this book up to this section is useless until you take action. Action is key. Far too many people spend too much time researching and forecasting and trying to better understand the market and end up achieving very little. They go around in circles until they're stuck in paralysis by analysis. Until you take action and actually invest, nothing is really achieved. You might have improved your understanding, but you haven't improved your financial position whatsoever.

Of course, there is a process involved. You need to understand your current situation. You need to understand the fundamentals of property investment, but then you actually need to implement. This section,

Understanding Implementation, will give you an overview of how to action your knowledge; from how to finance your properties and the tax rules, to accounting and how to manage your portfolio as it grows.

CHAPTER SIX

Finance

Property is an attractive investment opportunity mainly because it gives you the ability to leverage your money. In this chapter you will find out about how important it is to understand the financing of your property investment, how to use investment debt to grow your property portfolio, the different types of mortgages available to you, and why you need to use a broker to find the right deal for you. When investing in property, the investor must decide whether to take finance or purchase using just cash.

Without finance, property is relatively bland. The returns are not great from cash-bought property due to the costs of holding the asset, resulting in average net returns usually between 6% to 10% per annum when considering both yield and growth. The choice you make is usually determined by what you hope to achieve from the investment. You will remember reading about this when you set goals in Chapter 4. This is where your property investment strategy and goals come into play. Borrowings are used to accelerate returns by applying a deposit and leveraging it with further funds. Generally, this is for capital growth, however if the interest rate is lower than the rental yield, then it can also accelerate income returns.

The fact that you can take a 25% deposit, for example, and buy a £100,000 property with £25,000, essentially quadrupling your money, means that even if the returns on the total asset value are relatively average, the returns on your cash will be quite strong.

With property you can borrow relatively high loan to values (LTV) over the long term. The average maximum LTV in the UK is 75%, meaning the LTV that most lenders will go to without hiking up interest rates. At the time of writing this book, interest rates are still cost effective with no ability for the lender to recall the mortgage unless you do something wrong, regardless of the value of the property going up or down.

There is no other investment asset class where you can do this. You can borrow to invest in shares, but it's very costly and risky because you get margin calls if the value of your share portfolio falls, which means you end up selling or putting in more cash at the worst possible time. This does not happen with property. You can keep your property for the full mortgage term regardless of what happens to the value. That is what makes property attractive: by leveraging your money four times, if you achieve an average 5% capital growth return on the asset value, you will get a 20% return on your cash. The UK average for the past twenty years is 5.5% per annum, so 5% is very achievable. In the current market, we aim for a 10% plus net yield on the funds applied. Using the same example as above, if you apply £25,000 and buy a £100,000 property, we would aim to achieve £2,500 plus per annum after all expenses and pre-tax. If you add those two figures together, 10% from cash flow plus 20% from the growth, you're at 30% plus returns per annum on your cash without setting the world on fire on the asset value and with quite strong confidence in achieving that return. No other investment option offers 30% returns with low risk.

As a potential property investor, you need to understand this because the prudent use of investment debt, which is what mortgages are, is essential for people to achieve their goals. Most people could save every penny they possibly can over their lifetime and still not have enough money to retire comfortably. The ability to leverage that money means you can better utilise it and make it go further. Another word for this is 'gearing'. Rather than buying one £100,000 property for cash and achieving 5% or 6% returns per annum, you could buy four with that same amount of money and quadruple your returns. To have cash-bought property is an under-utilisation of your money, especially when borrowings are so cheap at the moment. When you can borrow at 2% or 3% and achieve yields of 7% or 8%, then add into that the growth, you are under-utilising your resources by not leveraging or gearing your property.

To best utilise property investment you need to understand how it applies to your personal situation. Firstly, it's vital to understand the types of mortgages available to you.

Types of mortgages

1. Residential mortgages

   This is the mortgage that most people are familiar with. It's the mortgage on your home. It's solely for the purpose of living in the property, and the serviceability for that mortgage is your personal income. The banks will want to know everything about you including your inside leg measurement (well not quite) when you go for a residential mortgage because they want to be sure you can meet the repayments. Their considerations will include your age, earnings, credit history and monthly expenses. These mortgages are also heavily regulated.

2. Buy to let mortgages

This type of mortgage is quite different. They are considered commercial mortgages as opposed to consumer mortgages because they are used for the purpose of business. The business is investing in property. These mortgage lenders are more focused on the property that you are buying and the yield that that property provides as opposed to your personal situation, as it is the rental income that services the mortgage. These mortgages aren't as regulated as residential mortgages and tend to be more flexible and more easily obtained.

It's vital that you're aware of the tax changes that have come into effect with buy to let mortgages in recent years. I will go into these in depth in the next chapter, but to summarise, until this year buy to let mortgage interest was treated as a deductible expense, therefore a tax deductible cost. This has been phased out for individuals who own properties in their own name and are higher rate tax payers. The wording of the change can be misleading, but essentially by 2021 buy to let mortgages are deductible at 20%, though as a tax credit rather than a deductible expense. This means that because the basic rate of tax is 20%, if you are a basic rate tax payer, you're not affected by this legislation. It's only higher rate tax payers that are affected as it means they can only deduct about half of the mortgage interest they were previously able to.

Approaching a lender

There is a broad range of lenders in the market. On one end of the scale you have high street lenders who are generally the cheapest but also the most restrictive. Quite often they will want you to have a minimum income and to tick several boxes to be able to deal with them, both with regards to your own situation and the property that you are mortgaging. At the other end of the scale are expensive lenders that will lend to almost anyone. Then there's a broad range in between with a number of specialist lenders for certain types of people and property.

As a borrower, it's important to be aware that the Prudential Regulatory Authority (PRA), which is an arm of the Bank of England, recently mandated that all buy to let lenders need to use a benchmark rate of 5.5%. This is the level at which lenders need to stress test your mortgage. For example, if you're borrowing £100,000 at 2%, and the property you are buying easily covers that cost, the lender needs to stress test it at 5.5% to make sure it also covers that cost in case rates increase. What complicates this calculation slightly is that it now needs to cover both the 5.5% interest rate and it needs to cover it 125% of the time to account for vacancy periods and extra cost. A quick calculation below to explain further:

Monthly rent = £1,000

Yearly rent therefore = £12,000

Amount that can be borrowed
$$= 12,000 / 0.055 / 1.25 = £174,545$$

I will go into these changes in more detail in the next chapter. But for those with lower yields of sub 5%, this can mean that they can no longer borrow as much as they previously could. Take London as an example, where properties are generally high-value and low yield. Since the changes, the average maximum borrowing loan to value is about 55% to 60% for buy to let, based on the above stress test formula whereas previously it was 75% plus. The old strategy of buying a property and just breaking even solely for growth doesn't work as well any longer because you can't borrow as much.

This makes London a tough market because average prices are £500,000 plus. You need to contribute at least £200,000 to buy a property that is probably just breaking even from a cash flow perspective. If the yield is only neutral then your main purpose for investing is growth in a market that has already grown quite a lot. That creates challenges in high-value, low yield properties, whereas it doesn't affect lower-value, high-yield properties as much, because the yields are substantial enough to support the borrowing. It's important for you to be aware of this and how it might affect you, your strategy and your current portfolio. One way around this issue is to use five-year fixed term products which are exempt from the new servicing rules. However, that means that you're locked in for that period of time unless you pay high exit fees which restrict your ability to re-mortgage and build on your portfolio.

There are also changes with regards to portfolio landlords, which are defined as a landlord with four or more properties, excluding their home. In 2017 it was mandated that all lenders needed to look at a portfolio landlord's whole portfolio as opposed to just the property they are re-mortgaging, to ensure that it was profitable and passed the necessary stress tests. As a consequence of this new legislation, portfolio landlords now need to provide a cash flow analysis and a business plan before they are accepted for a new mortgage. This emphasises the benefits of dealing with a good independent mortgage broker, because a broker will be able to tell you exactly what information you need to provide as opposed to going to a lender and having to do it all yourself. There are a range of lenders who specialise in portfolio landlords, and each have implemented the changes slightly differently, so it's important to be aware of all requirements, interest rates, and the terms and loan to value differences across that spectrum.

There are over 1,000 buy to let products available in the UK at the moment, and over half of these are available through intermediaries or brokers only. By trying to manage this process yourself, you're immediately cut off from half the market. Many people new to investment make the mistake of speaking to their local bank about a buy to let mortgage. Then they get turned down or only offered the products that particular bank has to offer. That means that they're only offered one or two of the thousands of available options out there. Quite often, the high street bank is not the right lender for them. And if they say 'no', then that person might think that they can't get a mortgage, which just simply isn't true.

This illustrates the benefits of dealing with an independent, qualified, and experienced mortgage advisor that can actually look at the whole market and determine which lender has the most suitable products and best deal for you. Mortgage advice is one of our core services at Nova because we recognise for the ordinary property investor, this is a critical point to get right. Not only is it an inefficient use of a property investor's time, but they don't have access to the software or the information to be able to make informed decisions – which is why most people use brokers.

Using a broker

You need to be careful when using a broker, as there are many different types of brokers out there. For example, there are very big companies where there is often a lack of real personal service. Advisors are likely to be young and with less experience, and have been taught to follow the company's scripted process of mortgage advice. Then there are the specialists who are divided into residential mortgage specialists and buy to let specialists.

Be warned that the broker doesn't do buy to let mortgages all the time they won't be familiar with all of the products and lenders on the market, and won't be able to provide as good advice as a specialist in that area. Not only that, but specialists are familiar with the terms and conditions associated with buy to let mortgages and will be able to guide you appropriately.

Don't go for the cheapest broker. Some brokers don't charge fees, which often means they chase the highest commissions from lenders. Other brokers charge quite high fees, and while I recommend being careful of this too, don't be afraid to pay good money for good advice. As with anything, you get what you pay for. If it's going to cost you £1,000 to get a £500,000 mortgage, the right mortgage could save you tens of thousands of pounds over the mortgage term and the right broker could save you a lot of headaches while arranging it.

This is where your long term goal, which I spoke about in an earlier chapter, comes into play. You might want to build a property portfolio and build equity in your properties so that you can re-mortgage them in two or three years' time to re-invest in further properties. But if your broker has signed you up to a fixed five-year product, you'll have to pay exit fees if you want to re-mortgage before the five years are up. Think of your strategy before you sign on the dotted line, because you don't want to be locked into something if you want to sell that property or re-mortgage it before the end of your mortgage product term. You could end up paying several thousands of pounds in exit fees.

Your broker needs to know your goal and have the experience to advise you on choosing the right product to meet that goal. At Nova we aim to ensure that property selection, finance and tax all work together to meet your strategy and this is where a lot of people go wrong. Make sure you're clear on what you want to achieve, and have a set criteria, to actually get the right finance product in place before you start.

To summarise, my top tips for choosing a broker are:

1. Choose a specialist in their field and check reviews or get referrals from friends or other professionals you trust

2. Make sure they know your goal for that particular property and long term goal so that they can choose the right product for you

3. Do your research so that you choose the right broker for you

Expat and overseas buyer mortgages

There are mortgage products available for you to buy property in the UK even if you live abroad. An expat is someone from the UK who is now living overseas but the term 'expat mortgages' is also often used for overseas buyers who aren't from the UK. The expat mortgage market has grown a lot over recent years, whether buying a residential home in the UK that isn't currently occupied, or purchasing a buy to let property.

As an expat you are far better off using a UK-based broker as generally the products will be from UK-based lenders. In saying that, the likes of Bank of China will do expat mortgages. They are a UK lender, but they're not a UK bank. We would also advise using an expat UK mortgage specialist as the criteria can be stricter for expats and overseas investors. An expat will generally need a slightly higher income than a standard buy to let mortgage. You might need to already have a credit footprint in the UK too, or perhaps some assets in the UK already. There are more boxes to tick, but there are certainly options available. For overseas buyers, it also depends on their personal and financial situation and the country they live as to whether mortgages are an option.

Depending on where you live, there will also be tax implications. The UK government generally collects 20% tax through agents from people who live outside the UK. For example, if you are in Australia, there is a tax treaty with Australia where you're able to claim that back as a tax credit, assuming you were an Australian tax resident, whereas if you are a UK tax resident, you would pay your tax in the UK. It's important to get the correct advice if this is your situation.

CASE STUDY

Why use finance?

John and Adam both have £200,000 to invest. John uses finance and buys four properties worth £200,000 each with a 75% mortgage. Adam buys one property worth £200,000 with his cash and no finance.

John's likely returns: Drivers; 6% yield per annum (pa), 3% interest rate pa, 5% capital growth pa, average costs

Total NET yield over 10 years	£280,680
Total NET capital growth over 10 year	£664,584
Total Return (yield plus growth) over 10 years	£945,264
Total percentage return on funds applied	472%

Adam's likely returns: Drivers; 6% yield pa, 5% capital growth pa, average costs

Total NET yield over 10 years	£114,873
Total NET capital growth over 10 year	£166,146
Total Return over 10 years	£281,019
Total percentage return on funds applied	140%

All numbers are pre-tax. The reason John's returns significantly outweigh Adam's is the cost of borrowing is only 3%, but the returns are significantly more. So by borrowing, John better utilises his money than Adam. Hence the value to leveraged property investment.

What have you learned?

We have reviewed the benefits of leverage in multiplying returns and better utilising your resources to achieve your goals, recent changes in the UK mortgage market and the importance of considering your long term goal when choosing your mortgage product to prevent getting caught with exit fees (such as if you sell your property before the end of the mortgage).

Some of the many buy to let mortgages will only be available through a mortgage broker.

It's important to choose a buy to let specialist broker to ensure you get the best deal and enable you to reach your goal.

As an expat or overseas buyer, you must also seek specialist advice: use a UK-based broker who will know the deals available to you. Investing as an expat means you must be aware of specific tax implications depending on your country of residence: work with a tax advisor who can help you navigate the tax rules.

Questions for you

1. If you currently own buy to let properties, what is your loan to value ratio? You can work this out by dividing the loan amount by the value.

2. If it's below 75%, could you be better utilising the equity in those properties to build on your portfolio?

3. Do you use a broker for your mortgages?

4. If you are just getting started, can you see the benefits in maximising borrowing and using a specialist broker?

5. Are you familiar with the recent changes related to buy to let mortgages? For more info go to www.nova.financial

Please do take our Property Investor Scorecard and determine your Property IQ at: www.nova.financial/ scorecard

In the next chapter we will cover the importance of tax structuring and accounting. Often this is neglected by property investors who find it boring or too complicated to understand. But this is a mistake. While I would recommend that you always use an expert for tax and accounting, having a good understanding of tax legislation and how it affects your property portfolio is vital if you want to sustain your successful investments.

CHAPTER SEVEN

Right Tax Structuring And Accounting

To most property investors, tax and accounting can be boring topics and they get put off trying to understand it. But I have good news for you. You don't need to fully understand it so long as you have the right advisors or the right specialist property accountant in place but you should have a general understanding of what they're doing for you. A good advisor should be able to explain things in easy-to-understand terms. Getting the correct advice will have a big impact on the net funds you are actually putting in your pocket. Obviously, we are always seeking the best returns possible, and are looking to maximise the use of our resources. However, before you put returns in your own pocket, you have to figure out how much tax you're going to have to pay on them. That is what is so important about tax and accounting.

No one likes paying tax. But paying tax is a good problem to have because it means you are making money. You have to have the right tax structure in place to make sure that you are mitigating tax. You only pay tax when you have a profit, and it should be looked at that way. You shouldn't, as the old saying goes, 'let the tax tail wag the investment dog'. Don't go into an investment solely for tax benefits. Many of the 'tax efficient investments' have been sold on this basis and failed because they were being offered for tax benefits as opposed to the actual fundamentals of the investment.

Firstly, you want to make as much money as possible and structure that in a tax effective way so that you can mitigate the tax you pay on those profits. To do this you need to start by learning about the different types of tax in relation to property. This is not intended to be an in depth look into tax, but more an overview as a starting point or refresher.

Types of property taxes

There are several different types of property tax that you will need to be aware of – Stamp Duty Land Tax, Income Tax, Capital Gains Tax and Inheritance Tax. I will give you an overview of each, but I recommended you look for an experts' advice as you go forward.

1. Stamp Duty Land Tax (SDLT)

   This is the tax you pay on purchasing property, or the tax that the government makes on a property transaction. The amount you pay depends on the value of the property you buy and on whether it's your first property: recent changes have introduced a Stamp Duty premium of 3% for subsequent property purchases. This premium was introduced by the Chancellor to raise funds for the Help To Buy scheme where the government lends new buyers up to 20% outside London and 40% inside greater London towards the cost of their newly built home as an equity loan, so they will only need a 5% cash deposit and a 55% or 75% mortgage to make up the rest. See the Stamp Duty Threshold table below.

Property Price £	SDLT rate %	SDLT surcharge rate %
Up to 40,000	0	0
40,001–125,000	0	3
125,001–250,000	2	5
250,001–950,000	5	8
950,001–1.5m	10	13
1.5m Plus	12	15

2. Income tax

   This is very similar to employment PAYE tax and is levied at your marginal tax rate. As it currently stands in 2018, if you're earning less than £46,350 a year, you're a basic rate taxpayer at 20%. If you earn between £46,351 and £150,000, you're a higher rate taxpayer at 40%, and if you're earning £150,000 plus you will pay a rate of 45%. With property, this is levied on the net profit. That net is then added to your current marginal tax rate. However, there has been another change recently, which is called Section 24. This refers to the way that buy to let mortgage interest is tax deductible against the rental income of a property. The wording of the legislation is confusing as it suggests that once in full effect, mortgage interest will not be tax deductible at all. However, so long as the individual's income from both employment and their properties is less than the higher rate tax payer's threshold, your tax position will not actually change. Quite often we meet married couples that have one high income earner and one low income earner. In this case, income can be diverted to the low income earner for tax efficiency and in some cases to avoid the impact of Section 24. This is done by submitting what is called a Form 17 to HMRC. Again, seek advice as this is often overlooked.

By 2021 mortgage interest will be no longer deductible, but a tax credit will be given at the basic rate of 20%. If you earn more than the higher rate threshold and own properties in your own name with mortgages, the debt will be less tax efficient. It's important to note too that these changes will be phased in up to the 2021 tax year. At the time of writing in late 2018, the Chancellor recently announced changes to the higher rate tax payer threshold, increasing it to £50,000 in April 2019: meaning that you will only be affected by Section 24 if you earn over that amount. For a married couple that is generating solely property income, this means £50,000 each per annum – a total of £100,000 – to stay on the basic rate of tax and often avoid the impact of Section 24. I'm sure you can see that it is worth getting expert tax advice to determine how this will affect you personally.

3. Capital Gains Tax (CGT)

This is the tax payable on any net gains on the sale of a property. The taxable amount is calculated using the following formula:

Sale price – Purchase price – Capital costs = Capital Gain that is taxable

This equation gives the net gain. The following is an example:

If you bought a property for £100,000 with £10,000 of capital costs (such as Stamp Duty, legal fees and renovations, etc) and sold for £200,000, then you've got a gain of £90,000. That £90,000 will be taxable at either 18% (if you're a basic rate taxpayer) or 28% (if you're a higher rate taxpayer). There were some changes brought in recently with regard to capital gains tax which reduced the rates, but residential property is exempt from those changes.

4. Inheritance Tax (IHT)

This is effectively a tax on the wealthy (or what is considered the wealthy) as you do receive an exemption up to a £325,000 and anything over that is taxed. The standard Inheritance Tax rate is 40%. It's only charged on the part of your estate that is above the threshold. For example, if your estate is worth £500,000 and your tax free threshold is £325,000, then the Inheritance Tax charged will be 40% of £175,000 (£500,000 minus £325,000). There are numerous ways of protecting funds and assets from IHT or to mitigate it (which are beyond the scope of this book) but again, seek the advice of a specialist advisor.

Of course, if you're an expat looking to buy property in the UK you will need to consider, based on where you live, what the tax thresholds and taxes you are going to incur. UK tax will be automatically levied on you, but if that country has a tax treaty with the UK you may get credits for it. Or you may be able to arrange with the HMRC to pay tax in the country you currently live in, for example. You will need specialist expert tax advice on this.

It's clearly very important to structure your purchases in the most tax efficient way possible, as it can be quite difficult to 'unscramble the egg' once you've bought one way and try to change that ownership structure. For example, there are lots of people at the moment who are higher rate taxpayers who own properties in their own names with high levels of debt, and will be hurt quite badly by the Section 24 changes. They will be looking at how they can change that ownership structure. Let's look at the ownership structures available to you.

Types of ownership structures

There are several different ways to structure the ownership of your property portfolio:

1. Personal name

2. Limited company

3. Limited Liabilities Partnerships

4. Trust Structure

5. Hybrid structure

Below is a brief description and explanation of each. But first – a disclaimer; this section is not intended as advice and is not specific to you. It's intended as an overview for general information and you should seek professional advice before choosing what structure is right for you.

Personal name

The traditional way of owning property is in your own name, and that's how the majority of buy to let property is owned. However, spurred on by the Section 24 changes, there has been quite a big shift in the market, especially for new purchases. The move is now away from owning in your own name towards ownership in a Special Purpose Vehicle (SPV) limited company. If, however, you're a basic rate taxpayer or if you can divert income to a partner's name on a basic rate tax threshold, you're better off in your own name because your tax rate is only 20% and the income goes straight to you providing more flexibility.

If you're married, you can fill in what is called a Form 17, as one partner in the marriage may be earning a high income and one may be earning little or no income at all. You can then divert property income to the lower income earner's name. The ideal scenario, depending on the wealth of the couple, is that each of them is earning just under the higher rate tax threshold per year making them both basic rate taxpayers. Once they both go above that, then they may be better off assessing other ownership structures.

Limited Company Special Purpose Vehicle (SPV)

Before Section 24 was announced, only 5% of new buy to let mortgage applications were for limited companies, and in the final quarter of 2017, nearly 70% were. You will want to think carefully before you set up a limited company to invest in property and assess the advantages and disadvantages before you do.

Advantages of limited company structures:

1. Limited companies are, at the time of writing, exempt from Section 24, so buy to let mortgage interest remains fully tax deductible as an expense. As a higher rate taxpayer, it can be more tax efficient to have properties in a limited company.

2. It can be tax efficient to have funds in a limited company and keep the money there as the current tax rate in a limited company is 19% and will be coming down to 17% in 2020. However, this doesn't suit everyone as taking the money out of the company, especially if you are paying Corporation Tax and then paying salary or dividend tax, means you're essentially being double taxed and that is not very tax efficient.

3. This option can work well for people who want to build an asset base within the company while working or having other income outside of the company. This is on the basis that in ten or fifteen years' time they will scale back their employment and therefore their tax rate. It then becomes more tax efficient to draw down funds from the company when you don't have much in the way of other income. It's more of a long term wealth creation strategy rather than a 'retire tomorrow' strategy.

4. Finally, if the funds for investing are coming from outside of that company structure initially, you can lend the money in the form of a director's loan to the company. Let's say

for example, you have £100,000 in your own name. You set up the company for the purpose of investing in property. You lend the money to the company. This is then a loan on the balance sheet from you to the company, and you can pay that £100,000 back however you please, tax free. For example, £10,000 a year for ten years. This is a good option for someone who wants some income from their limited company but is on a higher rate of tax. They can draw down on that loan from the property income in the company and effectively view it as income while not actually drawing an income for tax purposes and therefore effectively kicking the ball down the field before they need to pay tax on drawings from the company.

Disadvantages of limited company structures:

1. In the future Section 24 could be applied to limited companies.

2. A limited company locks your funds up and then you do need to try to get them out somehow. But there are tax efficient ways of doing this depending on your tax position outside of the company and your stage of life.

3. A limited company that is used for passive investment is classed as an investment company, meaning that essentially you invest the money and it just sits there. It's similar to a dormant

investment company that is fully liable for Inheritance Tax at 40%, whereas if it's a trading company, it's exempt. The definition of a trading company is a company that is actually actively doing business. For example, if you're heavily involved in managing your properties and/or renovating them, as opposed to the business being a passive vehicle, then you can be exemption from the Inheritance Tax. This is a specialist area, and you should definitely seek advice on that before making any sort of assumptions.

Limited Liability Partnership (LLP)

LLPs can be used by property owners as a structure for purchasing property, or properties that are owned in your personal name can be transitioned into an LLP. There are various reasons as to why one might use this ownership structure, most of which is beyond the scope of this book. If you're a professional landlord with mortgaged properties in your own name, then this structure may be worth assessing and you should seek professional specialist advice before doing so. Remember though, ownership structures should be selected on the basis of making good business sense, not just for the purpose of mitigating tax.

Trust structure

With this structure there is a trustee who is responsible for managing the assets of the Trust, and a beneficiary who is the person who benefits from the Trust. They're often used for minors or for inheritance purposes if someone is under the age of twenty-one or for people who are not mentally sound or trustworthy. They're also used to protect assets from divorces and litigation. For property ownership, Trusts are quite limiting as it's difficult to get mortgages for this kind of structure. However, for tax purposes, there are quite a lot of very creative ways of mitigating tax through trust structures. Grosvenor Estate is a mainstream example where, quite recently, the Duke of Westminster died and passed on his estate to his son who paid very little if any tax on billions of pounds worth of assets. But for your regular investor, in general, trusts are not very beneficial for building or maintaining a property portfolio.

Hybrid structures

There are an infinite combinations of hybrid structures. Since Section 24 was announced, various structures have been created and utilised. Hybrid means a combination of two or more. An example of a hybrid structure is a Limited Liability Partnership (LLP) which transitions into a Trust with the beneficiary being a limited company. Structures like this are generally used for tax purposes. If you decide to investigate hybrid structures further, then you will need to take expert advice to ensure what you do is completely legal and ideally covered by an advisors professional indemnity insurance in case HMRC decide the structure you have used is not legal or breaks tax rules.

Remember, the right structure for you will have a lot to do with your strategy, what your stage of life is and your level of wealth. There's not a one fits all solution. For example, a young person with £50,000 to invest who is a higher rate taxpayer and is going to be working for the next thirty years but wants to build a property portfolio on the side will want a very different structure to a sixty-year-old couple who have £3,000,000 in cash and want to retire tomorrow.

I can't stress enough the importance of seeking professional advice from specialists. A trusted tax advisor is essential to your successful property ownership. If you think any of these structures are suitable for you, be sure to visit your accountant (if they're adequately qualified in property knowledge) to discuss your needs and what's best for you. Use an accountant who specialises in property, as a general practice accountant will not be able to give you the detailed advice you need to make the right decisions as you grow your property portfolio. If you don't have a property specialist accountant, feel free to get in touch using the contact details provided at the end of this book and I will personally direct you to one.

CASE STUDY

The difference between the right tax structure and the wrong one can make a substantial difference the amount of post-tax money you keep.

For example: John is earning £150,000 per annum and is therefore in the 45% tax band. If John generates property income of £50,000 per annum on top of that, then he will pay 45% on that income and be affected by Section 24. However, if John has a wife, Wendy, that doesn't earn any money, simply by filling in a Form 17 and allocating the property income to Wendy as the beneficiary of that income, they would pay a mix of no tax and 20% tax and likely not be affected by Section 24 at all.

That's a likely savings of between £10,000 and £30,000 per annum, a big difference for a little change. There are various examples of this so please do seek advice.

What have you learned?

In this chapter we have learned that paying tax is good as it means you're making profit but you want to mitigate the amount you pay through tax planning, and that there are several different types of tax you will need to be aware of:

1. Stamp Duty

2. Income Tax

3. Capital Gains Tax

4. Inheritance Tax

Once you understand the types of tax you might need to pay, you will want to decide on your ownership structure.

The ownership structures we have discussed in this chapter are:

1. Personal name

2. Limited company

3. Limited Liabilities Partnerships

4. Trust Structure

5. Hybrid structure

The structure you decide upon is unique to you and your decision will be based on your overall strategy.

Questions for you

1. Are you a current landlord and if so what ownership structure have you utilised?

2. Do you have a specialist property accountant? If not, get one!

3. Were you aware of the different ownership structures?

4. Which do you think might work best for you?

5. Are you a current landlord and have you assessed how Section 24 will affect you? If not, you need to as soon as possible.

6. Have you assessed how the different types of tax will affect your net return?

Once you've decided on the type of ownership structure that is best for you, the next step is to manage and grow your portfolio. In the next chapter we will cover how to review your performance and make decisions about re-investing your profits in new properties, and importantly, how to set up a management structure that will suit your lifestyle and enable you to become a passive property investor.

CHAPTER EIGHT

Managing Your Portfolio

As your property portfolio grows you will want to ensure you implement effective management processes which will allow you to

1. Evaluate your investments regularly

2. Re-invest to grow your portfolio further

3. Implement the passive investment model

This chapter deals with how to set up those processes. We will look at the steps to reviewing your investments, and how to re-invest successfully. We will also cover the key management model which enables you to continue being a passive investor. This is the model we prefer our clients to set up. In case you want to be more involved in the day to day management of your properties, I have also included other models for you to consider.

Review and re-invest

Review and re-invest is crucial to becoming a successful passive property investor. We've discussed earlier in this book the importance of understanding your goals and having a strategy for achieving them. However, having goals is one thing, you then need to take action. Once you begin to build your portfolio, you then need to review where you stand at various stages to make sure you're continuously working towards the goals you want to achieve.

I see review and re-invest as taking multiple actions, not just one. When it comes to investing in property, it's usually not just a one-off event, unless, of course, you've got a big inheritance or a windfall of some sort that's given you enough cash to invest and achieve the passive income goal that you need from day one. But that doesn't happen to everyone. Reviewing and re-investing are going to be essential to actually getting towards your end goal.

At Nova we say that any property investment should be looked at as a seven- to ten-year investment. That's because the property market is cyclical and a relatively slow moving. But that's a good thing as it means there's not really a bad time to invest so long as you are in it for the medium to long term.

Ideally you want to re-mortgage every two to three years to release equity and re-invest. For example, let's say you buy a £100,000 property with a 25% deposit, then three years down the line it's worth £125,000. You now have £50,000 equity in the property, of which £31,250 could be released through a 75% mortgage at the new value and then re-invested in a second property. This would allow you to buy another property of a similar value to the first. Of course there would likely be some fees associated with the remortage process, but that's likely to be circa £2,000 and easily covered by the new investment.

Property can provide a snowball effect, and given the scenario I've just described I'm sure you can imagine two properties becoming four, four becoming eight and eight becoming sixteen. You can see how your investment grows in Appendix 1 Building a Portfolio for Retirement.

Ideally, we're aiming to create equity, re-mortgage, re-invest, and keep building the portfolio with each of the properties being cash flow positive, and then we're not only building on the equity but building on the cash flow as well. That enables us to build the size of the portfolio, the net investable asset base, and then also the passive income which is the end goal.

Steps to reviewing

With mortgages in the UK, you will generally have an initial period of two to three years. This means that a bank might lend to you at a rate of 2%, but it's only at 2% for two or three years and then it goes to the revert rate which is usually about double that. Often people will stay with that lender for the initial period, and then they will re-mortgage either with the current lender or with a different lender to get another initial rate.

This gives you the opportunity to find out what your property's worth and whether there's the equity there to pull out. This means that we're almost forced into the position of reviewing and re-investing every two to three years. There's always the option of going for longer initial periods, of five years for example, but that means you will often be locked in for that period. This option will only make sense if you don't want to review and re-invest sooner.

To re-invest effectively you need to:

1. Speak with an independent specialist broker

2. Find out what your options are

3. Identify the current interest rates

4. Apply that to your particular situation and your property

5. Get specialist property advice

6. Do your own research on where the market is at that point in time

By doing this it's as if you've gone full circle. You started with your investment, gained some equity, then reviewed and re-invested by applying your research and due diligence. Make sure to find out if the market is still the same. Should you be investing in a similar location, or has the market moved on and changed? Should you be investing somewhere new?

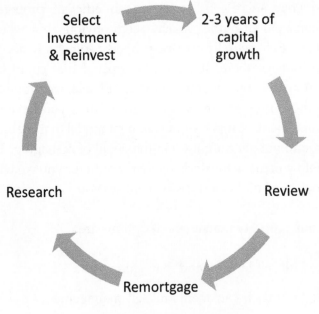

Select
Investment
& Reinvest

2-3 years of
capital
growth

Research

Review

Remortgage

Fig 8.1:Top tips for re-investing

1. Don't diversify just for the sake of it. Look at different types of properties and different areas only if there are good quality investments available, and not just for the sake of diversifying to spread risk.

2. Don't procrastinate. Implement. Until you act you haven't really achieved anything.

Property management

Whether you have one property or several, the key to your success is to set up an efficient property management model. It may seem obvious, but when it comes to actually owning property, somebody needs to manage them. It would be great if that could be automated, but in reality, it can't. At Nova, we promote passive property investment. To do that, you have to implement a property management model that enables you to not get caught up in the detail of managing. To help you make the decision that is right for you we will look at all of the options available to you.

Your property management options are:

1. Full self lettings and management

2. Lettings by an agent and self-management

3. Lettings by you but an agent manages your properties

4. Full lettings and management by an agent

You have the option of self-managing property, meaning you have to find your own tenants and manage those tenants throughout the tenancy period. If, for example, the dishwasher stops working, the tenant will call you straightaway. You will then need to arrange to get the dishwasher fixed. In this management model it's the responsibility of the property owner to organise and fix anything that goes wrong, unless it's maliciously done by the tenant.

Self-management can work, but I'd encourage you to be an investor as opposed to a landlord. Some people want to be more hands on, and they even pride themselves on being a handy landlord. This means that they're out visiting their properties all the time. They might even do the work themselves. I don't recommend this option as it's time consuming and not really a great use of your time unless you have a large portfolio close to home and you're willing to make it your 'job'. Some people are professional landlords. That is what they do for a living. Their properties might be near where they live, making them easier to self-manage. In this scenario it can make sense to have a self-management model to a certain extent, but obviously one person can only do so much, especially depending on the size of their portfolio, how much maintenance is involved in the properties and how passive or active they might be.

However, at Nova we encourage property as a passive vehicle for wealth creation. We look at it in a very similar way to investing in shares. If you invest in Apple, you're not expected to maintain Apple's office. We encourage our clients to have a management team in place. This is often referred to as a Power Team. And it becomes even more important if your properties are not close to where you live.

This is becoming more and more the case in the UK, especially for people who live in London and the southeast where it's becoming more difficult to find good property investment opportunities. They're investing in areas like the Midlands and the Northwest which might be hours from where they live. If you have the right management structure in place, then you would never even have to see your property. Often people like to be able to see their properties from a comfort perspective, but remember, we're being commercially minded and unemotional about our investments, and they should be where it makes the most financial sense to be as an investment and make money and not just close to home because you'd like to feel 'warm and fuzzy' every time you drive past them.

Building a Power Team

If you decide the self-management model is not for you, you will need to build an effective Power Team around you who can respond quickly and effectively to the needs of your tenants without you having to get involved. The Power Team can take a number of different forms, but essentially you need a reliable and experienced property manager. Quite often, if you're investing in centrally located developments of property, like an apartment building with management services, the property manager will be the onsite at the development.

This is the ideal scenario, as it means there's a manager available around the clock who can respond most of, if not all, the time. For example, quite few years ago I lived in Brisbane and rented in a building of four blocks of flats where the manager of the building also lived. He was able to give an almost immediate response to call-outs from the tenants. This made things really easy for the tenants and the landlords, since if anything went wrong, you just went down, knocked on his door and it was sorted very quickly. There was no need to wait for an agent that might be miles away. Having onsite management will mean you can be passive in the ownership of your property and leave your Power Team to deal with the everyday issues raised by your tenants.

A good property manager can help you build your Power Team through their network of contacts. This is particularly important if you own older properties that require more maintenance. Your manager should have a handyman on call and the right contractors such as electricians, plumbers, etc, that they can rely on to do the right thing on service and price for you.

It's well known in the industry that agents will get kick-backs from local contractors. So you will need to do your due diligence. Read online reviews and forums and speak with other landlords in the area to find people you can trust in a particular location. Make sure your property manager is a member of the right industry body and has the right qualifications and experience. It's also important to ensure that they are not overstretching themselves. Some agents or property managers could be managing up to 200 properties per person, which can mean that it will take them a long time to do anything, because they are going to have a very long list of things to do.

Full lettings and management by an agent

You can also choose to implement the full lettings and management by an agent model. This is a package of management services for your properties, which means you can be fully hands off with your portfolio. You do this through employing the services of a lettings and management agent. The agent will help you find tenants, and provide the management and maintenance of the property. This is a particularly good model if you own new properties, as the maintenance will be low. Once you have a tenant in place, the whole burden of management will be taken away from you as the investor as opposed to the landlord.

You can, of course, choose a combination of any of these management models and create something that works effectively for you. You could do your own lettings, find new tenants and self-manage your properties. Or you could use an agent just for lettings but continue to manage the properties yourself. You could also do the lettings yourself but use an agent or property manager for the day to day management of your properties.

My view, and therefore that of my advisory business, is that it is best to utilise a full lettings and management model and use an agent for the whole process. This requires having the right agent in place to allow you to be hands off.

Management fees

Management fees can vary quite substantially. For example, some of the bigger agents in London charge up to 20% for full lettings and management. Outside of London you are looking at 8% to 10% for full lettings and management. Property investors and landlords are realising that the margins in property management have been out of hand for far too long, especially with bigger agents who have charged much higher fees, and we are now seeing a lot of lower cost agents entering the market. These can be Internet based and the actual hands on services are outsourced to local agents in the area.

You will want to consider the option that is best for you and get the right balance between cost and getting the work done effectively. At Nova we encourage all of our property investors to be commercially minded. Although full management comes at a cost, so long as we've accounted for the costs within our cash flow and we're happy with the net outcome after accounting for that cost, then implementing a full lettings and management model is the best way forward.

Assured short hold tenancy agreements

It's not the purpose of this book to go into the minutiae of tenancy agreements and contracts, however it's important that as a property investor you understand what is involved in a tenancy agreement. Usually these are for six to twelve months. Landlords tend to prefer a year-long contract as it means you have tenants locked into the agreement for that full twelve month period.

There are a whole range of rules and regulations around tenancy, and it's worth getting some education on that as a property owner. A good source of information is landlord associations which tend to focus on the information you need to know to be compliant when you rent out properties in certain areas. You will be kept up to date with current regulations and requirements, such as the requirements for energy performance certification in properties (EPC) which you need to have done every ten years.

One thing that is very important is to confirm employment details and seek references for potential new tenants to make sure that they can actually afford to pay the rent and have a record of doing so. Taking a deposit of a number of weeks' rent is essential and means that if the tenant stops paying or if they break something, then you can use that deposit to make up the short fall. The last thing you want is to end up taking a tenant to court because they don't pay and you need to evict them from your property. This can be very costly, especially if you have a mortgage in place and therefore repayments to make.

This is also why it's important to be confident that you're dealing with a quality, reputable agent – and perhaps don't hand over the reins completely. Make sure you're comfortable with the tenants that are going into your properties as well. It's important to keep in mind that agents are remunerated on actually having someone in your property. You want to make sure they are putting the right tenants in your properties and not just people who may stop paying their rent, as it will be you who pays the consequences for those bad decisions.

One way of mitigating that risk is to have landlord's insurance that covers lost rent and eviction costs. It's quite cheap at about £200 to £400 a year depending on the property. And quite often this insurance will provide cover if your tenant stops paying and you're forced to take them to court to get them out. Check your policy though, as not all of them do. Again, you should discuss this with a specialist landlord insurance broker, some mortgage brokers are able to do this to get the right policy in place. Make certain it covers you for damage, lost rent and legal fees at the very least.

As a rule, you want your rent to increase over the years. The rental component of Consumer Price Index (CPI) has been substantially higher than CPI itself for quite some time, meaning that rents on average are rising much quicker than people's incomes. This does raise the question of whether rents are becoming unaffordable but again, as an investor, you are doing this to make money so you do want to make sure that your rents are increasing in line with the market.

The increase usually happens with the renewal of the tenancy agreement. You should seek advice about what that increment might be from either the agent or from a company like Nova that is helping you build your portfolio and create that wealth. An easy way of determining the amount is to look at what similar properties in the area are renting for. If your rent is below that, then you are justified in increasing it.

Of course, if you set the rent too high you will soon know as your property will not rent readily. If you have vacancy periods or your viewings are low that means, compared to the market, you're charging too much. And that applies to the sale of property as well. Far too many people are quite emotional about the 'value of their property' or how much it 'should' rent for, and if you remove the emotion, it's the market that determines your rent and value not what you think. There's no point in having a property empty, especially if dropping your rent by a small amount will mean it rents all the time. Keep your finger on the pulse because having slightly less rent for twelve months is better than having rent for only six months of the year.

CASE STUDY

Some property investors like to invest close to home solely to save on management fees or so they can keep an eye on their property. However, if the return on properties outside of your home area is substantial enough to outweigh the cost of management and save you the time of doing it yourself, would you not be better off?

Also, with a good management team in place, why would you ever want to check on your property? It won't have disappeared, and an agent can send you up to date pictures regardless of where you're located. This may be slightly different to conventional thinking, but it is logical.

A good example of this is properties in London versus properties in Manchester. At the time of writing in 2018, the average rental yield in London is circa 3.5% and the average yield in Manchester circa 6%. So if you live in London and want your Manchester property fully managed, it will cost you about 10% of your rent, but the overall yield is nearly double so well worth it.

What have you learned?

Reviewing and re-investing is essential when building an investable asset base. This is an ongoing cycle which enables you to value your property, release equity and re-invest in more property to grow your portfolio, your investable asset base, and your passive income. Taking action here both initially and on an ongoing basis is crucial.

As your portfolio grows you will need to decide on the right management model to put in place. We encourage our clients to implement a full lettings and management package so that they can get on with being investors rather than getting caught up in the day to day requirements of managing their properties.

You will need to do your research to choose the right agents and build an effective Power Team around you so your properties are managed efficiently.

Questions for you

1. Are you a current landlord and do you review and re-invest every two to three years?

2. If you have not invested yet, what is stopping you? Take action!

3. Have you sought advice on the right strategy for you on an ongoing basis?

4. What management model do you/will you use?

5. Do you see the benefits of full lettings and management so long as the cost is accounted for and the net returns are still acceptable?

CHAPTER NINE

Business Owners Investing In Property

At Nova we find a lot of our clients are business owners, whose business is doing reasonably well to the point where they have been able to accumulate spare funds. This usually starts out as a buffer for their business, but then grows beyond what is needed for working capital, plus a buffer. The size of this financial cushion obviously depends on their business, but it grows to the point when essentially it is sitting there achieving very little, sometimes in a UK business bank account achieving only 1% interest, if even that.

Lord Alan Sugar recently said in *The Guardian* newspaper that property investment is the best hedge against business.[17] What he meant by this is that property investment is a great way of diversifying. He also said in an article in *The Telegraph* newspaper in 2017, 'You make money from property and do business for fun',[18] meaning that once you diversify, you can often make more money from property than your original business. This has certainly been the case for Lord Sugar, as although he started out in consumer electronics, the vast majority of his billionaire wealth these days is made from and stored in property. I think we can all agree that Lord Sugar knows a thing or two about business and making money, so we should probably heed his words.

If you're not yet a business owner, don't worry as this chapter is still relevant. Given that you're reading this book, I will assume that you at least plan to build an investable asset base, perhaps through property investment, and you will therefore be a business owner soon. This is why I have chosen to include this chapter specifically for business owners who might be wondering what they can do as their business profits grow.

Essentially, this means converting your proactive business profits or income into passive income, to the

---

17 Sugar, A. 'Lord Sugar tells his Apprentice to invest in property if he wants to be wealthy in business'. *The Telegraph,* January 2019 www. telegraph.co.uk/finance/enterprise/11929491/Lord-Sugar-tells-his-Apprentice-to-invest-in-property-if-he-wants-to-be-wealthy-in-business.html
18 Sugar, A. 'Lord Sugar enjoys £181m dividend property empire'. *The Telegraph,* January 2017

point where you have a portfolio of properties either within your existing company or within a company that is separate to it, but associated with it. This portfolio now provides you with income, and ideally capital growth, on your investment asset base. If there is an economic downturn and your business slows, or even folds, you will have something else that you have created through your proactive business activities. This is referred to as diversification or a hedge to your business. I look at my passive investments as 'forever money', which not only diversifies the risk but makes me feel a lot more comfortable about it as even if everything I've worked so hard for in business 'goes belly up', I still have them.

It's quite a common strategy to move profits or your proactive income into passive investments that give a good return. And the interesting thing about leveraged property investment, which we have covered in previous chapters, is the fact that by achieving relatively average returns on the asset value, you can be achieving 30% plus returns on your cash, which in some cases might be a better return than your actual business generates. This is considered a supplement or a hedge to your business, and it might get to a stage where property investment is a more lucrative, viable and flexible business than your original business activities.

Three ways to invest in property as a business owner

There are three main ways in which a business owner can invest business funds in property. They can:

1. Invest through their existing company

2. Establish a Special Purpose Vehicle (SPV) and lend the money across from the existing company and invest

3. Establish a Directors' Pension or a Small Self-administered Scheme (SSAS)

Many business owners structure their income or their total drawings (salary plus dividends) from their company in a fairly tax efficient way. They aim to minimise the overall tax payable, setting it at a point where they're not paying too much tax, or get to a point where they are comfortable with the amount of tax they are paying.

This could mean they're left with extra funds in the company that is profit, but that they don't want to pull out yet as they are likely to be taxed 40% on those funds (the higher rate tax band for people earning more than £50,000 per annum as of April 2019). The money often sits there and they're not really sure what to do with it, especially since they're busy running their business. One solution is to invest the funds in property through your existing company. In doing so you purchase a property in the existing limited company, with leverage or not, but of course leverage does allow you to better utilise your funds.

This is quite straight forward as the company already exists. However, there are two potential downsides to this option. Firstly, by investing within your existing company, you expose the investments to your existing company's risks. If your existing company starts to struggle, has liabilities and becomes insolvent, that could affect the investments. Secondly, some lenders prefer to lend to Special Purpose Vehicle (SPV) property investment companies for the aforementioned reason.

Special Purpose Vehicles (SPVs)

Many lenders prefer property investments through a limited company are done through a Special Purpose Vehicle, or SPV company. This is essentially a company set up solely for the purpose of investing in property. This is the most common strategy for utilising business funds.

Banks prefer this aspect of investment being split from the business as it separates the risk. For example, if I own a launderette that has loads of debt, and then it goes to liquidation or becomes insolvent, and I have the properties in there as well, that could risk the properties because it's within the one entity. If it's separate, the property is completely safe. And it's safer for the investor as well. By having a separate SPV limited company you do exactly that. You separate your risks.

Using my launderette company, I can set up my SPV and lend the money across. If I own 100% of both companies, or even my wife and I or my business partners and I own 100% of both companies, we can lend the money across to the other company that we also own as a commercial loan.

You should pay a nominal rate of interest rate back to your original company, but that doesn't matter because you own both companies anyway. And this is a great way to better leverage under-utilised business funds while not having to take the funds out of the tax effective limited company structure. Many business owners are not aware of this option.

At Nova we have a lot of business owners who come to us with large sums of money sitting in their business accounts that have accumulated over time. While they have been focusing on their business, they've ended up with a big pot of money that they're doing very little with and that could make a huge difference to helping them achieve their lifestyle and financial goals, as well as providing a hedge against downside risk of the existing business.

Director's pensions

Director's pensions are often referred to as Small Self-Administered Scheme (SSAS) pensions. I host a TV show called *Proper Wealth* on Sky Channel 189 for Property TV, and recently I recorded an episode about this very subject. You can watch the episode here: https://nova.financial/videos/proper-wealth-ep14-directors-pensions-kevin-whelan-director-of-wealthbuilders

You'll find the full range of our videos via this link: www.nova.financial/properwealth

Director's Pensions are described as the best kept secret in financial services. This is because you become the trustee of your own fund rather than trusting someone you don't know, and you're taking your pension funds out of the system. At the moment, most people's pensions are managed by fund managers and financial advisors. They most like you to stick with that option as it keeps the funds in their control and they can charge you yearly advisory fees. The problem with this option is that most funds underperform the market and the fees are so high that people don't even really think of their pension as theirs. Hence, Director's Pensions are not widely advertised.

But there's another option for business owners only that allows you to better utilise the money, and that is Director's Pensions or a SSAS which is a Small Self-Administered Scheme. By doing this you essentially take control of that money. You set up your own structure. You can, in fact lend up to 50% of the funds to your own limited company for investment. What's more, you can lend the whole lot out to unrelated parties if you want to. Or you can simply invest it yourself through the tax free pension structure that you've created, quite often in lower cost funds than are available in the traditional pensions.

This makes Directors' Pensions very flexible and tax efficient. They are better than tax efficient because they're tax free. Based upon current legislation in 2018, business owners can contribute up to £40,000 per annum as a salary sacrifice to their pension, so it's quite easily built up quickly. You can contribute up to £1,030,000 over your lifetime, which is inflation linked so likely to increase each year. For a business owner who wants to invest in property, develop property, or simply to invest in a whole range of investment activities with full flexibility and control, they can set up this structure. They can contribute to their pension yearly and essentially generate tax free returns.

A word of caution. This can only be done by people with business experience. You need to prove that you own your own business and be approved by HMRC. But as I said before, many people are not familiar with this and don't know this option is available. A lot of people we talk to at Nova don't really think of their pension money as theirs. It's just this other pot of money that they've been contributing to for years and they're not really sure what it's worth or when they're going to get it. But by utilising this structure, you can actually take control of it and use it to contribute to your financial strategy and goals, rather than just leaving it up to somebody else.

The business owners' mindset

As a successful business owner, you probably already have a commercial mindset simply because you're operating a business. Running a business requires you to be commercially minded and unemotional about what you're doing to be successful. You're probably used to the idea of putting in place goals, developing a strategy and then implementing that strategy.

This is a process that is more familiar to business owners than it is to others, in general. A business owner who doesn't diversify and utilise their excess profits is not doing themselves any favours. In fact, they're shooting themselves in the foot. It's very easy to get complacent when you've been successful – but what happens if, for whatever reason, there's a downturn in your business? It's while you're successful that you need to use your extra resources for property investment, otherwise you're wasting a valuable opportunity.

It's important to note that lending for buy to let mortgages through limited companies has become a lot more cost effective and a lot more competitive. There are many more products available on the market now, and this has been somewhat driven by Section 24. Section 24 has resulted in many more people investing through limited companies, and quite often for tax reasons. And it's not just business owners who are doing it, but people who are higher rate tax payers who are trying to avoid Section 24. This does work in the favour of business owners investing their extra funds within their business, as it means that there are a lot more options available.

We frequently get asked about mortgage options by business owners who want to diversify into property investment. Although you may be a savvy and successful business owner, when it comes to investing your profits in property, it's still important for you to seek advice on the implementation of a strategy, investment selection, and the right ownership and financing strategy for you and your goals.

You may be a successful plumber, but you probably don't have all the knowledge you need about finances and investments. My advice is to get an expert's specialist help in this area. The same goes for property selection and on implementing a mortgage. It makes sense to seek advice from people who may know what you may not know.

Commercial vs residential property

Investing in commercial properties as a business owner is a sensible idea if you're buying your own premises and are confident that you're going to be a long term tenant of that premises yourself. The Director's Pension option can be a great way of helping you achieve this by providing you with the funds you didn't know you had access to. This is only so long as you can afford it and you can get cost effective finance in place, and, of course, if it makes sense for your business. But I would advise that unless it's your own premises, to think that a commercial property is better for you just because you're a business owner is not necessarily true.

At Nova we generally focus more on residential property because the interest rates are much lower, the loan to value ratios are generally higher (more borrowings and less deposit), and the vacancy rates are much lower. Although the yield on residential properties is often slightly lower than on commercial property, it's not uncommon for commercial properties to be empty for six to twelve months or more between tenants, whereas residential can be a matter of days in the right circumstances.

With commercial properties, if you've taken a mortgage at a higher interest rate and a lower loan to value, you'll be applying more cash, and you have higher repayments. You need to be able to afford that potential vacancy period. Most people, especially when they're starting out (unless they are already quite wealthy) probably can't afford that liability or don't want to take that sort of risk.

Commercial property is higher risk. It's also generally expensive to buy good commercial properties in good areas. In general, commercial property makes more sense to people who are already well above average wealthy, rather than people who are looking to build their asset base with a certain level of confidence.

Property management

Finally, a word on passive property management. You'll remember from Chapter 8 the following list of options available to you to manage your properties effectively:

1. Full self lettings and management

2. Lettings by an agent and self-management

3. Letting by you and agent manages

4. Full lettings and management by an agent

As a successful business owner, I don't recommend you opt to do full self lettings and self-management. In fact, I would strongly suggest that you go for the final option on the list – full lettings and management by an agent. Most business owners are busy people, and they want to focus on their main business. They're utilising property investment as a hedge and as a way of building passive income and their asset base alongside their proactive business. They really want their properties to be as passive as possible, and just tick along and help them build an investable asset base without them having two or more jobs.

You want property investment to work alongside your main business, so you need to make sure you're following a passive investment model. That means you're not having to devote time to getting your feet caught in the weeds of day to day property management.

To summarise this chapter, as a successful business owner with a growing pot of money, one way to use this pot is to diversify and invest in property. At Nova, we support business owners through the decision-making process and what the best strategy and structure is, all with the end goal in mind.

Deciding on whether residential or commercial property is a good option for you is very much dependent on whether you can afford a good premises in a good area, and whether you will be the long term tenant on the site. We also advise that regardless of how successful you are, you seek advice from an expert on the best way forward for you. This could be through a range of different structures, depending on your situation and your goals. Either way, you need to speak to an expert to ensure you're making the right decision for you and your business.

What have you learned?

Property investment is an excellent way to diversify if you're a successful business owner with a growing pot of unused cash. There are three main ways in which a business owner can invest in property:

1. Through their existing company

2. Through a Special Purpose Vehicle and lending the money across from the existing company

3. By establishing a Directors Pension or a SSAS to utilise pension funds.

What's right for you will depend on your situation and your goals, and you should seek expert advice to find out what your options are.

Investing in commercial property versus residential property is dependent on whether you have the funds to buy a good property in a good area, whether you will be the long term tenant at the site, your level of wealth, and your risk tolerance.

Finally, the preferred way to manage your properties is through a reputable agent to be responsible for lettings and full management of your portfolio, and allow your portfolio to be passive.

Questions for you

1. Do you have excess funds in your business that could be better utilised?

2. Did you know that you could invest in leveraged property through your business using one of the three mentioned structures?

3. What is the current return on capital in your business? Does it beat the 30%+ you could achieve from leveraged property investment?

4. Do you have any diversification or hedging against your business going through bad times?

5. Do you see the value in diversifying into property investment?

6. Did you know about Directors' Pensions? Is it worth finding out more?

Having created such wealth for yourself, you can think about the social responsibility we have, not only our local communities, but globally as well. In the next chapter we will cover how we can use your profits to give back to society and to help others who are less fortunate than ourselves. I will tell you about the ways in which you can reach out to others and the importance of doing this for you, your staff and your company.

CHAPTER TEN
Giving Back

Now that you have a framework for creating wealth, what's important is a strong sense of social responsibility and giving back to those less fortunate than us. We are very privileged to live in a developed country with unlimited opportunities, whereas more than half the world lives in developing countries with very few opportunities. When you consider that all you need is a laptop and the Internet to do well in business these days, we can perhaps pat ourselves on the back as it has never been easier to make money.

However, there are significant portions of the world that this is unavailable to. I personally and my colleagues at Nova Financial Group think it's important to help ease the pain of others in greater need.

In this chapter we will cover how we at Nova give back to society and how you can follow suit if you see fit. We will also cover the impact that giving to charity can have on your business as a whole. I hope that by the end of this chapter you will be able to see how important it is and how giving back, rather than affecting your bottom line, can actually have a positive benefit on both your own happiness and success, as well as help maintain a positive reputation and a strong level of social responsibility.

At Nova we work with a great charitable organisation called Buy One Give One, which enables small to medium sized businesses to contribute to a vast range of different charities with a variety of causes. You can find out more about the charity by visiting their website www.b1g1.com/businessforgood.

This charity underpins each transaction or action we take at Nova. For example, every time a client invests in a property through us, we provide a year of housing to people who are homeless in India. Every time we send an email, we donate a litre of water to people in need in Ethiopia. And we send thousands of emails a month, so you can imagine how many litres that adds up to! At the time of writing, we have clients investing in more than thirty properties a month, so we know we are making a pretty big impact on the lives of a large number of people. We're doing this without really hurting our bottom line, as the contribution that Buy One Get One aims for is 1% of revenue (an even smaller fraction of profit) from small to medium sized business owners and contributions are completely tax deductible. And it's not just business owners who can do this. Individuals can also work with this charity as well.

Although we advocate you taking a business approach to property investment, it's still easy to contribute a small portion of your property profits towards charity. There is an abundance of charities that you can work with –though it's important to do your research and due diligence into each charity. Don't just give your money to anyone.

We've teamed up with Buy One Give One on the recommendation of another business that we were comfortable and confident with. The charity fits our organisational values, and you should make the same decision for your business. It's important to seek out referrals from other business owners or property investors and review each charity in depth to make sure that your money is actually going to good use.

The impact of giving back

If you do not do it already, once you align your business with a charity and start giving back you will find that this simple strategy creates a wave of positivity and a sense of achievement and purpose throughout your employees. They will see that they're working for a business that is not just contributing towards its own gain. If you're a business that has sales teams, then giving to a charity can be very powerful when you take targets away from revenue, and attach them to 'giving' opportunities instead.

For example, at Nova we have recently changed our Key Performance Indicators (KPIs), to the number of houses we build for our charity. This is a completely different mindset. We want our guys to have that strong sense of social responsibility. We want them to feel good about helping our clients, but also know that by generating revenue for the business, they're helping others as well. That is what changing our KPIs has achieved – employees that want to make the business successful so that they can help those less fortunate than themselves.

There are several other ways in which giving to charity will help your business:

1. It builds respect for your brand.

   We let our clients know they're providing a year of housing whenever they invest through us. It doesn't just make us feel good. It doesn't just make our staff feel good. It makes our clients feel good as well. It's not just philanthropy, it also makes you feel fantastic about what you're doing on a daily basis. This all contributes to your brand reputation, as your property business will become known as one that gives back rather than just existing to build a profit.

2. **Contributions from a business to charity are tax exempted.**

Any contributions your business donates to a charity will be tax exempt. And from an individual to a charity, there is Gift Aid, where the government contributes extra on top of your contribution.

3. **It helps recruitment and staff retention.**

People will join your organisation and stay with you if the values of your business match their personal ones. One of those values may be to give back to those in need. Staff often want to know that they're working for a business that is not all about making money. They value knowing that in some way, through their work, they're also having an impact on poorer communities. This helps you to attract good talent to your team because they can see that there is a meaning and a purpose to the business, as opposed to just making a profit. Today's workforce, especially millennials, believe this is more important than any generation before.

4. **You can help several charities by fundraising in short bursts.**

It may not be ideal to support only one charity. In fact, you may find it appeals more to your staff if they know they can support a variety of charities throughout the year. And this needn't hurt your bottom line. At Nova we got involved in Movember, raising money for men's health such as mental health support and cancer awareness. We raised over £500 in November 2018 simply by growing moustaches for the month (and women can do 'Move to Movember' which is about walking or running for the cause). A short-term campaign like this is easy and costs nothing. Staff choose to run marathons, swim miles or bike the Himalayas for their favourite charities. By supporting these staff with your contributions, you're not only making your staff feel valued, you're helping those in need.

To conclude, consider how you can give back and make charitable donations to help others. Not only will this enhance your business reputation, it will help you recruit better talent and more importantly, retain staff. It will make you and your staff feel good that the work you do is having a positive impact on others less well-off in society.

What have you learned?

Giving to charity ought to be part of your business strategy once you can afford it. This will help build your brand reputation, boost recruitment and staff retention, and make you and your staff feel great about the work you do.

Questions for you

1. How could you give back at the moment?

2. Have you checked out the Buy One give One website? Here it is again: www.b1g1.com/businessforgood.

3. If you can't afford to give back just yet, do you see the value of doing so once you have built more wealth?

4. Do you think you could participate in fundraising events like Movember to raise money as well or instead of ongoing donations?

You've now come to the end of reading about my approach to passive property investment. I hope you've found the book useful and are ready to take action and start investing in your first property or taking a more strategic approach to building your portfolio. If you would like advice on how to move forward, you will find all of my contact details and that of my advisory business in the next section. And as a valued reader of my book I have a great offer to help you get started. All you need to give is some of your time.

And that's a wrap! So what should you take away?

Property is often the largest purchase you will ever make in your life, with the current UK average property price circa £225,000. Most people don't spend that sort of money every day, and it shouldn't be taken lightly. Despite this, property investment tends to be a very do-it-yourself activity or at least it has been in the past, which for me is difficult to understand. I would like to think that my level of understanding of property and investments is slightly higher than your average person through years advising others, investing myself, and over a decade of study – but even I wouldn't make such a large decision without seeking the advice of others who know what they are talking about and are independent in their advice. Humans are emotional creatures, and I've been saved from many bad decisions simply by using a trusted advisor as a sounding board which allowed me to see reason beyond the blinkers I had on at the time without realising it.

That is why I wrote this book. It's for people just like you who want to learn more about passive property investment. As a property investor for years myself, and now working with clients to help them develop a successful property portfolio, I'm very familiar with the mistakes people can make. But I'd like you to learn from those mistakes so you can go on to build a successful property portfolio.

What you now know

Now that you've read this book you understand our approach and methodology at Nova Financial Group, which we use with our clients on their property investment journey. We see buying a property as being very similar to researching a medical problem. You have to get expert advice. If you had a medical problem, you wouldn't self-diagnose. You would seek the help of a professional, a doctor who specialises in the illness you are suffering from who can help you and guide you in the right direction towards wellness.

It's the same with property investment. You must build your Power Team around you so you can draw on the advice of experts to understand any risks you are taking and make the right decisions for you, your goals and your future. When you're sick you go to the doctor, to do your taxes you go to an accountant, and when investing in property you should seek specialist professional advice.

You learned about the RETIRE Investment Journey which helps you plan for your retirement so you're financially independent. We've covered how to set your goals and the importance of having that Investors Mindset to make decisions about your portfolio with a business rather than an emotional mindset. I've taken you through the key steps to buying the right property:

1. How to do due diligence

2. Choosing the right mortgage for you

3. Finding a good broker and use them effectively

We have dealt with the issues of tax structuring and accounting, and how to continue to manage your portfolio in a way that allows you to continue to invest without getting caught in the day to day issues of property management.

At the end of reading this book, you know the key steps you can take to start to build a successful property portfolio.

But what do you need to do next?

Next steps

You now need to take action and put what you've learned into practice. Ensure that when seeking advice that you meet with a company that is independent and not just selling products or investments. I'm a strong believer that prescription without diagnosis is malpractice, and by this I mean you need to seek the advice of a company or person who takes the time to very clearly understand your situation, goals and preference prior to providing advice. Avoid those that advertise specific investment options or products, as more often than not that is what you are going to end up with.

Also, be wary of those that try to convince you of investment options that are completely outside of your comfort zone. It really doesn't matter how much sense an investment makes on a spreadsheet, if you're not comfortable with it after understanding all the reasons it might make sense, if you're going to be awake at night worrying about it then it's not right for you. Although some advisors will show you fancy graphs and stats to back up their advice. You've probably heard of the phrase 'a man convinced against his will is of the same opinion still'. Don't let the hype fool you into something you're not OK with.

The property industry, unfortunately, tends to be very sales focused. This means when it comes to making a purchase you're often dealing with a salesperson in the form of an estate agent or property marketer. The difference between sales and advice is that advice focusses on benefits, whereas sales focusses on features. When dealing with an estate agent they will often tell you how great the property is because it has a south west facing garden and a period fireplace. But do those things really matter? In some cases, these things might matter, like if that is what your target market wants. But how does that relate to you? That is where advice becomes very useful, as good advice focusses on benefits specific to you and your goals. Another way of putting it is focusing on the outcomes rather than the offering.

That is where my company, Nova Financial Group can help. We can help you make the right decisions to reach your goals. As a valued reader of my book, I feel like we now know each other quite a bit more, so I'd like to offer you a special promotion to help you take action and implement the points we have covered.

Nova has offices in Central London, Manchester & Birmingham, and we offer complimentary meetings to determine if we can assist. At that point, we usually charge an engagement fee of £500 to £2,500 depending on the complexity of your situation and the work we need to put into providing you with the right advice.

I'm going to waive that fee for you.

Get in touch, come in for a free meeting and if we can help we will provide advice to you on how you can improve your situation and implement the right strategy to achieve your goals. That is usually around ten hours of work specific to your situation, which will be completely free. There's a lot to gain and really not much to lose, aside from a little bit of your time.

If you would like to take advantage of this offer, or if you have any questions, you can contact me directly on my personal email: paul@nova.financial.

Or call Nova Financial Group on 0203 8000 600.

If you'd like to learn more about your current situation, investment strategy and how you can improve take our Property Investor's Scorecard to get an understanding of your Property IQ and where you stand, as well as any areas you may be able improve.

Contact us

If you would like to get in touch with us you can do that at:

⊕ www.nova.financial

🄵 @NovaFinancialUK

◻ @novafinancialgroup

Building a Portfolio for Retirement

What is achievable over 10 years from an average buy to let

Assumptions:

Property Value £200,000

Annual Growth 5%

Remortgaging at 25%

	Start with £50k investment	1	2	3	4
Property Value	£200,000	£210,000	£220,500	£231,525	£243,101
Initial Mortgage	£150,000	£150,000	£150,000	£150,000	£150,000
LTV	75%	71%	68%	65%	62%
Net Rent (2.5%)		£5,250	£5,513	£5,788	£6,078
Debt with Net rent repaid		£144,750	£139,238	£133,449	£127,372
LTV with NET rent repaid		69%	63%	58%	52%
75% of value		£157,500	£165,375	£173,644	£182,326
Equity up to 75%		£7,500	£15,375	£23,644	£32,326
Equity in %		4%	7%	10%	13%
Equity up to 75% with NET rent repaid		£12,750	£26,138	£40,194	£54,954
Equity in % with Net yield repaid		6%	12%	17%	23%

5	6	7	8	9	10	11
£255,256	£268,019	£281,420	£295,491	£310,266	£325,779	£342,068
£150,000	£150,000	£150,000	£150,000	£150,000	£150,000	£150,000
59%	56%	53%	51%	48%	46%	44%
£6,381	£6,700	£7,036	£7,387	£7,757	£8,144	£8,552
£120,990	£114,290	£107,254	£99,867	£92,111	£83,966	£75,414
47%	43%	38%	34%	30%	26%	22%
£191,442	£201,014	£211,065	£221,618	£232,699	£244,334	£256,551
£41,442	£51,014	£61,065	£71,618	£82,699	£94,334	£106,551
16%	19%	22%	24%	27%	29%	31%
£70,452	£86,724	£103,811	£121,751	£140,589	£160,368	£181,137
28%	32%	37%	41%	45%	49%	53%

The snowball effect of remortgaging and reinvesting in buy to let property

	Year 1	Year 5	Year 10	Year 15	Year 20	Year 25
Number of properties	1	2	4	8	16	32
Years from start to have debt free properties	18	23	28	33	38	43
Income assuming Average price of £481,324 debt free and 4% NET yield	£19,253	£38,400	£76,800	£153,600	£307,200	£614,400
If investor is 30 years of age the age they will be from investment to debt free passive income	48	53	58	63	68	73
Net asset base assuming average price of £481,324 and debt free	£481,324	£962,648	£1,925,295	£3,850,591	£7,701,182	£15,402,363
						31
						29
						27
						25
						23
						21
						19
						17
					15	15
					13	13
					11	11
					9	9
				7	7	7

Year 1	Year 5	Year 10	Year 15	Year 20	Year 25
			5	5	5
	3	3	3	3	3
	2	2	2	2	2
	2	2	2	2	2
Start with 1	1	1	1	1	1
		4	4	4	4
			6	6	6
			8	8	8
				10	10
				12	12
				14	14
				16	16
					18
					20
					22
					24
					26
					28
					30
					32

APPENDIX TWO

Resources

The Property Investor's Scorecard: www.nova.financial/scorecard

Proper Wealth (TV Show on Sky Property TV and available online 24/7 www.nova.financial/properwealth; also available as a podcast)

Property Question Time (TV Show on Sky and available online 24/7: www.nova.financial/propertyquestiontime)

Property Encyclopaedia: www.nova.financial/propertyencyclopaedia

www.walkscore.com

Tracker for house price trends by area: www.hometrack.com/uk

House price index: www.nationwide.co.uk/about/house-price-index

House price index: www.halifax.co.uk/media-centre/house-price-index

Office for National Statistics: www.ons.gov.uk

Credit report checker: www.checkmyfile.com

Credit report checker: www.noddle.co.uk

Online property website: www.rightmove.co.uk

Online property website and house prices statistics source: www.zoopla.co.uk

'Where Can I Afford to Rent or Buy?' housing calculator: www.bbc.co.uk/news/business-23234033

Sold prices and valuations search: www.mouseprice.com

The Telegraph/Savills 'Should You Rent or Buy?: www.telegraph.co.uk/finance/property/house-prices/10373797/Should-you-rent-or-buy.html

Data tool for property investors: www.propertydata.co.uk

Data tool for property investors: www.realyse.com

Video: How the Economic Machine Works by Ray Dalio, www.bridgewater.com/research-library/how-the-economic-machine-works/

Roomscan app: for creating floorplans

Further reading

These are helpful books to read or listen to to gain a business and investor's mindset:

Adams, S. *How to Fail at Almost Everything and Still Win* Big (2013, Penguin Group, New York)

Branson, R. *Finding my Virginity* (2018, Virgin Books, London)

Campbell, A. *Winners: And How They Succeed* (2015, Hutchinson, London)

Carnegie, D. *How to Win Friends and Influence People* (1998, Simon & Schuster, New York)

Chernow, R. *Titan: The Life of John D. Rockefeller Sr* (2004, Random House, New York)

Clason, G. S. *The Richest Man in Babylon* (1926, Penguin, NY)

Covey S. *The 7 Habits of Highly Successful People* (1989, Simon & Schuster, New York)

Ferriss, T. *Tools of Titans* (2016, Houghton Mifflin Harcourt, New York)

Goggins, D. *Can't Hurt Me: Master Your Mind and Defy the Odds* (2018, Scribe Media, New York)

Harnish, V. *Scaling Up: How a Few Companies Make It and Why Some Don't* (2014, Gazelles, Inc.)

Hoffman, R. and Yeh C. *Blitzscaling: The Lightning-Fast Path to Building Massively Valuable Companies* (2018, Crown Publishing Group, New York)

Kotler S. and Wheal J. *Stealing Fire* (2017, HarperCollins, New York)

Manson, M. *The Subtle Art of not Giving a F**** (2016, HarperCollins, New York)

Masterson, M. *Ready Fire Aim*: Zero to $100 Million in No Time Flat (2007, Wiley, New Jersey)

Peters, S. *The Chimp Paradox* (2012, Vermilion Books, London)

Priestley, D. *Oversubscribed: How to Get People Lining Up to Do Business with You* (2015, Capstone, London)

Reed, J. *Get Up to Speed With Online Marketing* (2013, Pearson, London)

Robbins, T. *Unshakeable: Your Financial Freedom Playbook* (2017, Simon & Schuster, New York)

Schwarzenegger, A. *Total Recall: My Unbelievably True Life Story* (2012, Simon & Schuster, New York)

Willink, J. *Extreme Ownership: How US Naval SEALs Lead and Win* (2015, Macmillan Publishers, New York)

Acknowledgements

First and foremost I must acknowledge my family; my wife, Libby, was a great support throughout the arduous process of writing this book and given that we gave birth to our beautiful daughter in the middle of it, she must be commended for always believing in me.

Secondly, to my parents who supported me as a child and throughout my schooling, without that I wouldn't be where I am today.

And lastly to my team at Nova Financial Group, as well as the many business leaders and colleagues that I work with on a daily basis; without learning from, relying on and helping each other, this book would never have been written.

The Author

Paul Mahoney grew up in a working-class town north of Sydney, Australia. His parents emigrated from the UK and Ireland a year before he was born. Both were self-employed, his father a mechanic and his mother a hairdresser. They weren't wealthy, but they worked hard. They lived week to week.

Despite this, they managed to send Paul to a private school where he was an enthusiastic sportsman with a specific focus on rugby and rowing. He then attended Sydney University to study Civil Engineering. But throughout all of his schooling Paul was never taught anything about money – the value of money, how to earn it, and what to do with it once he did. He discovered that nobody else learned about money either. They 'winged it' just like him. He worked full-time while attending University. He spent everything he earned.

Paul decided to change his studies to Financial Planning to learn about investments and personal finances. His ultimate goal was to become financially literate and then pass that knowledge onto others.

Paul learned about the options available to everyday people to improve their finances and applied this knowledge in various roles with Spring Financial Group across Australia. However, Paul spotted a gap in the financial services and property industries in Australia (and later in the United Kingdom), where financial and investment advice tended to be skewed towards equities such as shares, bonds and pensions. This generally ignores property as an investment option, resulting in very little advice available for property.

In 2014 Paul decided on a new business venture in the UK and partnered with a team of UK property experts to form the Advisory Panel at Nova Financial Group. Nova provides objective advice on finance and property, and specialise in guiding clients through their full property investment journey towards financial freedom.

Paul is a published author, keynote speaker and property expert/commentator. He is regularly featured in leading publications and on radio and TV and he presents at dozens of events each year across the UK and abroad. He is featured on the expert panel on Sky Property TV's *Property Question Time*, and he hosts a TV show (also on Sky) and Podcast called *Proper Wealth*, focused on wealth creation strategies including property investment. Paul's formal qualifications include Bachelor of Business (Financial Planning) with distinction, Diploma of Financial Services (Financial Planning), Certificate of Mortgage Advice & Practice (CeMap).

⊕ www.nova.financial

◼ @NovaFinancialUK

◉ @novafinancialgroup